# A HISTORY OF BAITCASTING IN AMERICA

Cornelia Marschall Smith (left) and Irene Marschall King fishing
in the Brazos River near Waco, 1910s

(Courtesy of the University of Texas at
San Antonio Libraries, Special Collections)

# A HISTORY OF BAITCASTING IN AMERICA

*By Emmett J. Babler*

*With a Foreword by Stan Fagerstrom*

# A HISTORY OF BAITCASTING IN AMERICA

by Emmett Babler

Graphic by Allen Aragon

Front cover illustration from the drawing Black Bass Fishing by A. B. Frost.

Back cover illustration from a 19th century Frankfort, Kentucky, street photograph taken at the door of the Milam fishing reel shop and kindly donated to the Capital City Museum in Frankfort by Willa McElroy "Billie Mac" Stagg Hoge. Photograph provided as a courtesy of the Capital City Museum, Frankfort, Kentucky.

Cover and book interior design by
Effusion Creative Solutions, Chandler, Arizona

First printing: 2017

Printed in the United States of America

ISBN   978-0-9989735-0-0

emmettbabler@gmail.com

baitcastinghistory.com

Big Papa's Bass Books image by Allen Aragon Gallery, Albuquerque, NM

# CONTENTS

FOREWORD — vii

PREFACE — ix

ACKNOWLEDGEMENTS — xi

1 ANGLING MIGRATES FROM THE BRITISH ISLES — Mid-1500s to 1800 — 1

2 KENTUCKY, WHERE BLACK BASS FISHING BECAME AN ART — 1775 to 1815 — 13

3 THE KENTUCKY BAITCASTING REEL — Mid-1830s to 1928 — 21

4 INDUSTRIALIZATION IN AMERICA — 1793 to 1893 — 33

5 MID-NINETEENTH-CENTURY BAITCASTING TACKLE — 1845 to 1880 — 45

6 TRANSITION TO BAITCASTING AS A SPORT — 1815 to 1881 — 57

7 A CODE OF AMERICAN SPORT ANGLING — 1850 to 1890 — 69

8 EVOLUTION OF THE SHORT BAITCASTING ROD — 1885 to 1920 — 79

9 NOTEWORTHY BAITCASTING LURES — 1883 to 1935 — 91

10 THE LAST KENTUCKY REEL MAKER — 1866 to 1948 — 105

11 TECHNOLOGY IMPROVES THE BAITCASTING SYSTEM — 1880 to 1960 — 117

12 THE BATTLE AGAINST BACKLASH — 1900 to 2016 — 127

13 ANGLING BOATS AND MOTORS — 1881 to 2016 — 141

14 EXPANDING THE POSSIBILITIES — 155

WORKS CITED — 161

A TRIBUTE TO STANLEY FAGERSTROM — 175

INDEX — 177

Lake Gogebic Michigan, Black Bass Fishing c1898

(Courtesy of the Library of Congress)

# FOREWORD

I've been around for a while.

If you're one of the millions of fishin' nuts who have been reading the "how to" stuff for most of the past century, you might recognize my name. Or for that matter, if you're not big on reading, you might have watched me do casting exhibitions at outdoor shows from Tulsa to Tokyo and from Birmingham to Brazil and countless spots in between for decades.

I actually was, you see, one of the old guys you read about now and then who caught his first fish on a bent safety pin because his folks didn't have the bucks to buy any hooks during the Great Depression.

I mention the above for just one reason. Having been plumb goofy about fishing since I learned to walk, and having been involved in the other stuff related to it all my adult life, I am occasionally inclined to form certain conclusions. There was a time when I might have had a tendency or two to think I was pretty knowledgeable about fishing and stuff related to it. Got a question? I'd have the answer.

How close to the truth was that? About as close as telling folks the next time you go out after largemouth bass you're gonna get a dozen ten-pounders. The truth of the matter is, I still encounter stuff today that makes me think I don't know my bass from a hole in the ground!

I met a man recently who brought this home to me in a hurry. His name is Emmett J. Babler. Like me, he's now living in Sun Lakes, Arizona. Emmett, a soft-spoken lifetime angler, has forgotten more when dealing with fishing in this great land than most of us will ever know.

If you doubt that now, you won't after you get very far into this book. It tells the story of a major part of American angling, from those hardy souls who were on the Mayflower right on down to the wondrous tools and tactics anglers can work with today. This book, as far as I know, is the only one ever written that details the history of baitcasting in the land of the free and the home of the brave.

How this book came about is a story in itself. Emmett's wife, Carmela, lost her father during the battle for Iwo Jima in World War II. Emmett had come by an abandoned tackle box that was of World War II vintage. It still contained much of the original tackle. One day Carmela, undoubtedly thinking about her father, asked Emmett if her dad once had a similar tackle box. Emmett replied that he probably did, because the lures in the abandoned box were from the same period.

Babler finally managed to come up with the missing contents for the abandoned box. Once he had it all filled and in top shape, he presented it to his wife in memory of her father.

The next questions his wife asked him are the reason you are holding this book in your hands today. First, Emmett's wife wanted to know what he planned to do with all of his gear when he passed on. When he told her he was going to give it to their grandchildren, she asked, "Do the grandchildren understand the significance and historical value of your gifts?" And before Emmett could answer, she suggested, "Why don't you write a book?"

I know a bit about writing books, because I've written four of them myself. But mine were all deeply connected to personal experience. Certainly Emmett Babler is an experienced angler, but adding one more how-to book to the thousands already out there wasn't what he was after. What he wanted—and as far as I'm concerned, has achieved—is something that's never been done before.

You are about to get a look at the result of the three years of dedicated and intensive research Emmett J. Babler has devoted to creating this book. A History of Baitcasting in America provides both the history of the sport and the intriguing stories behind the facts. This well-written and definitive angling source is a cinch to "hook" its share of interested readers.

I've been one of them, and I'm honored and pleased to have the opportunity to share my thoughts about it on these pages.

*—Stan Fagerstrom*

Stan Fagerstrom

Member of the Bass Fishing Hall of Fame and
the National Freshwater Fishing Hall of Fame

# PREFACE

My grandmother was a compelling storyteller, and when I was a boy, I loved listening intently to her as we sat around the table for hours at a time. Through her, history became much more than a collection of names and dates; it was alive. Somehow she transported people and events to us in that country-style kitchen of the old home and wove them into our lives. Although Grandmother did not fish, she would have liked the authentic story of how an angling method born in Kentucky developed into an American pastime and sport through the efforts of many individuals who recognized and acted upon the possibilities presented to them.

Individuals interested in exploring the origins and development of baitcasting in America may realize that books mentioning parts of its story are scarce and often were written in a much earlier era. Some readers who already possess an understanding of baitcasting history may have gleaned it from a variety of sources, ranging from old fishing books and periodicals to information published by tackle collectors, angling clubs, or countless Internet websites dedicated to all aspects of fishing. Until now, the sport has lacked a comprehensive single-volume history. My reason for writing this book is to provide that history as well as the fascinating stories behind the facts. Although obviously connected with fishing, the book documents the historical milieu that made American freshwater angling a possibility. My expectation for the reader is that this volume will become a helpful and trusted go-to source for baitcasting history, one you could perhaps let your grandmother read, even just for the story.

From its English origin and the days of King James I, when angling migrated to colonial America, to the frontier days of Kentucky where it became an art, baitcasting was poised to become a beneficiary of the Industrial Revolution and America's westward expansion. By the mid-1800s some of the country's most esteemed and influential citizens supported the new method of angling, and their advocacy guided the sport to national prominence. The availability of tackle originally handmade by gunsmiths, watchmakers, and silversmiths, and later mass-produced in the mid to late 1800s using business models employed by Apple a century later, fueled baitcasting's immense growth. By World War II baitcasting was the most popular angling sport in America. Following the war, development of newly engineered materials and advanced manufacturing processes further improved the baitcasting system and the watercraft that carried the anglers deploying it. In the twenty-first century, hundreds of thousands of Americans practice the now-global sport. I hope you enjoy reading about this history and find it as fascinating as I do.

A Morning's Catch in the Adirondacks

(Courtesy of the Library of Congress)

# ACKNOWLEDGMENTS

One person cannot compile a book of this scope. I would like to express my gratitude to the many people who assisted me with this endeavor.

First, I offer my sincere thanks to the United States Park Service, which maintains historic sites and landmarks throughout our nation. Park Service staff members at the following locations helped me discover much valuable information related to some of the key figures in the story of baitcasting and made appropriate photographs available.

The Martin Van Buren National Historic Site, 1013 Old Post Road, Kinderhook NY 12106

The Liberty Hall Historic Site, US National Historic Landmark, 202 Wilkinson Street, Frankfort, KY 40601

Ashland, the Henry Clay Estate, US National Historic Landmark, 120 Sycamore Road, Lexington, KY 40502

Additionally, I greatly appreciate the previously uncirculated photograph provided by Candace S. Shireman, Curator, Blair House, The President's Guest House, US Department of State, Office of the Chief of Protocol, Washington, DC. It contributed significantly to the visual impact of the personal relationships documented in Chapter 6.

I also wish to thank the staff at Johnson Hall, the New York State Historic Site located at 139 Hall Ave, Johnstown, NY 12095. The information and research leads obtained at this location helped immensely in documenting the colonial history of angling.

I am appreciative of the assistance provided by dedicated museum volunteers at regional and city museums. At each of the following locations, staff volunteers accompanied me on short field trips and provided local advice, photographic opportunities, and much valuable information.

The Skenesborough Museum, Skenesborough Drive, Whitehall, NY 12887. The hospitality extended by the museum volunteer staff was well above gracious.

Capital City Museum, 325 Ann Street, Frankfort, KY. I am indebted to the staff and volunteers, especially Lynda Sherrard, John Patrick Downs, and Eric Whisman, the museum's interface with the board of the Frankfort Cemetery.

Russ Hatter, known as "The Storykeeper of Frankfort, Kentucky," was an invaluable source for all information Kentucky. Without his help, this would have been a lesser book in both content and spirit. Russ provided a significant amount of research material that proved invaluable for documenting Kentucky's contribution to the sport of angling, and he kindly read and commented on my manuscript. Russ's devotion to Frankfort's history and his attitude to make the most of the possibilities life presents are infectious. At times when doubt set in about my progress on the book, I thought of Russ, and that kept me on track.

Polly Coblin, great-granddaughter of B. C. Milam, and Currey Gayle, great-grandson of Clarence Gayle, provided informal knowledge for which I am genuinely grateful; it improved, expanded, and cultivated the story of their famous artisan ancestors who were incredibly courageous, honorable, and community-serving individuals.

I offer a heartfelt thank you to Stan Fagerstrom, the honorable and most gracious angler and author who offered to write the foreword of this book. Many seek the attention of celebrated personalities such as Stan, and I feel privileged that he found the time to take me under his wing.

Kathy Carter, my editor, is not an angler, but when it comes to editing, she knows her stuff. A well-deserved round of applause goes to Kathy, who applied her editing skills so well to my manuscript.

Finally, I owe a great debt of gratitude to Carmela M. Hopkins, my wife and chief encourager. Carmela accompanied me on a month-long road trip necessary to complete both the colonial and early nineteenth-century research in New England and Kentucky. She supported my efforts for the past three years with patience, encouragement, and copious amounts of copyediting. I could not have written the book without her.

# Chapter 1
# ANGLING MIGRATES FROM THE BRITISH ISLES

*Mid-1500s to 1800*

## The Book of Sports

In 1618 King James I published a declaration, later known as the *Book of Sports*, that "was destined in after years to be one of the chief causes of a Sovereign and an Archbishop being dragged to the block" (1). Issued to stop Catholic and Puritan subjects from imposing their recreational restrictions on the king's Anglican Royalist supporters, the book identified both approved and prohibited sports in England; those approved were directed for use throughout the country on Sundays, a traditional day of leisure (1). Surprisingly, angling—fishing with a hook attached to a line typically connected to a rod—remained unlisted, a conspicuous exclusion.

Angling in Great Britain transcended social class, a reality unappreciated by nobles who found it difficult to maintain the sport's exclusivity. In practice, not theory, the upper class resented competition from commoners whom they considered illegal fishers or worse yet, thieves (2). The curious omission of angling from the king's book becomes understandable once the high esteem in which Britons generally held angling is recognized. In Britain, angling was not a game; it was "in no sense a fad or hobby" (3). Like hawking, hunting, and fouling, fishing was part of the British psyche—a passion, a sport, and an art—so angling remained unmentioned.

Britons may have found common ground with their shared love of angling; religion was another matter. The king's book had elicited significant Puritan anger throughout the country, not from opposition to leisure activities generally but rather from a concern about breaking the Christian Sunday Sabbath. For many Puritans, James's book "seemed a royal command to disobey" (4) the fourth commandment: "Keep the Sabbath day to sanctify it, as the Lord thy God hath commanded thee" (Deut. 5:12 KJV). As a result, tension increased between the Anglicans and Puritans. When James's son, Charles I, ascended the throne in 1625, he inherited a royal mess.

King Charles found himself as the head of a state-run church full of subjects who held assorted and conflicting religious beliefs, a powder keg that he failed to manage well. The inability of some subjects to exercise their religious faith freely had been a long-standing irritant, and Puritans wanted fundamental religious reform. In 1633 Charles I made a fatal mistake: he republished his father's *Book of Sports*, an action that drove the lower house of Parliament (The House of Commons) into a growing sympathy with the Puritans. Subsequently, because of the high level of animosity between the two parties, civil war ensued and the Royalists lost. In 1644 Parliament ordered the king's *Book of Sports* publicly burned, and on January 30, 1649, Charles lost his head.

## Angling Puritans

In September 1620, two years after James I published the first *Book of Sports*, about a hundred individuals, many of them Puritans in search of religious freedom, set sail for America aboard the *Mayflower*. They would become the Plymouth Colony in Massachusetts, the first permanent British settlement in New England.

Angling initially migrated from the isles of Britain to the Virginia Colony in America sometime prior to 1612 (5). However, it also traveled to New England on the *Mayflower* voyage or shortly thereafter, and it is most probable that Puritan anglers inaugurated the sport in New England. To some, this may appear an absurdity, considering the arguments over Sunday recreation in Britain and the long-perpetuated image of the hard-faced Puritan in American literature condemning colonial angling.

Various authors have proposed that Puritans were against all forms of recreation and back up their allegation by offering early New England colonial laws restricting leisure activities. As regards angling, this allegation is incorrect. Karl E. Johnson of Cornell University, in the study *Problematizing Puritan Play*, maintains that, contrary to what textbooks say regarding colonial law involving Puritan leisure, "blood sports were... discouraged by popular opinion, not by law. Also, untouched by legislation were other forms of 'legitimate' recreation, such as fishing and hunting" (6).

The reality is that in both England and America, the love of angling cut across social and religious lines, and Puritans were no more opposed to angling than the Catholics or Anglicans. Actually, some of the most renowned Puritan ministers of the sixteenth and seventeenth centuries were anglers.

In his legendary book *The Compleat Angler* (1653), Izaak Walton (1594–1683), a Royalist, informs us of the life of Dr. Alexander Nowell (1507–1602), an avid angler born during the time of King Henry VIII (1491–1547). (The quotation uses Walton's original spelling.)

I will content my self with two memorable men, that lived neer to our own time, whom I also take to have been ornaments to the Art of Angling.... The first is Doctor Nowel sometimes Dean of the Cathedral Church of Saint Paul in London... this good man was a dear lover and constant practiser of Angling.... [He] was observed to spend a tenth part of his time in Angling; and also... to bestow a tenth part of his revenue, and usually all the fish, amongst the poor.

What Walton did not mention is that the man he held so dear to his heart was a Puritan, albeit one who never separated himself from the clerical hierarchy of the Church of England. In 1553 Queen Mary I, a Catholic, exiled Nowell, and he took up residence with other reformers in Germany; there he came to espouse the views held by John Knox, quintessential Puritan reformer and founder of the Presbyterian Church of Scotland. After Mary died in 1558, Nowell returned to London as Dean of St. Paul's. Reportedly Nowell also invented bottled ale, an interesting disclosure for those with fixed notions about Puritan recreation (7).

The Reverend Thomas Foxcroft, a Harvard-educated Puritan minister who served Boston's First Church (Congregational) from 1717 until his death in 1789, published a homily in 1726 titled *A Serious Address to Those Who Unnecessarily Frequent the Tavern*. In the address, Foxcroft maintained Puritanism is consistent with recreation and advocated engagement in activities that would keep body and mind fit (8). Foxcroft obviously regarded an individual's decision to engage in sport as pragmatic and not principled or theologically driven. For instance, the reason Puritans did not engage in sports that involved violence or betting is that those activities were not productive. An excellent example of a sensible reason for Puritan angling, beyond nutritional interests or fitness, is that "the Puritans of New England supported fishing as a bonding experience for fathers and sons" (9).

## Settling the Connecticut River Valley

In 1633 the Plymouth Colony in Massachusetts dispatched William Holmes to erect a trading post at the confluence of the Connecticut and Farmington rivers. Leading a small group of colonists from Plymouth, Holmes sailed the Long Island Sound and then north up the Connecticut River about fifty miles to the farthest point navigable by seagoing vessels, the large falls. There he founded the first English settlement in Connecticut, the town of Matianuck (now Windsor, Connecticut). At this upstream river location, the settlement controlled trade to the north, where the Connecticut River starts flowing. And what an incredible river it was.

In colonial times, the mighty river was unspoiled by human intervention such as dams. It ran free, and its cold water was pure, untainted by industrial pollution. The river had been home to seemingly limitless numbers of Atlantic salmon who hatched there, found their way to the sea, and returned each spring to migrate upriver and spawn.

The earliest colonists along the river took to gathering below the falls with nets to harvest the seven- to twelve-pound fish. Hosts of salmon died with each drag of the nets, and queues of horse-drawn wagons lugged them away all day long for many days. The salmon were cleaned and packed into brine barrels to augment the sparse winter food stocks (10). This seasonal harvest remained a welcome sustenance activity every year until the salmon would stop running...and one day they did.

From the onset of colonial times, hunting and fishing were widespread in America; game and fish were numerous and their abundance taken for granted. However, it did not take long to realize that no indigenous population of fish and game could ever continue to support the human growth that was about to occur in the new country. Even in the smaller cities, it took but a short time to eradicate the local game surrounding the settlements (11). For the colonies to grow, development of an agricultural system was imperative; by Revolutionary times, that system was well established. Americans ate well even without the seasonal salmon harvest.

## Recreational Fishing Formally Appears in America

In 1732, the birth year of George Washington, recreational fishing formally appeared in America in the form of a fishing club near Philadelphia, a city founded by William Penn, a Quaker. Originally known as "The Schuylkill Fishing Company of the Colony in Schuylkill" and organized by distinguished city residents, the club featured fishing, hunting, and eating and drinking in a social atmosphere. Following the Revolutionary War, the club name changed from "Colony in Schuylkill" to "State of Schuylkill," for obvious reasons. Many of the original members, Quakers and emigrants with Penn to the New World (12), were respectably social and enjoyed leisure entertainment. Reportedly (although unmentioned in his diary), George Washington ate and imbibed at the Fishing Company on June 14, 1787, and the Marquis de Lafayette paid a visit on July 2, 1825, when he became an honorary member of the club (12).

"CASTLE" AND "HOUSE ON THE DELAWARE."

The Fishing Company's Delaware River location

The Fishing Company's clubhouse, known as the "Castle," was originally located on the west bank of the Schuylkill River near the present Girard Avenue Bridge. In 1822, as part of the Philadelphia waterworks project to improve the city's water supply, a dam was required; as a result, the river's swirling rapids became a big pond. The new dam also obstructed the upstream movement of fish from the tidal waters at the river's confluence with the Delaware Estuary, thereby depleting the fish population north of the dam. For those reasons, the Castle relocated to Rambo's Rock below the dam, where nothing obstructed fish movement. In 1887 a second relocation to the west bank of the Delaware River, about sixteen miles east of Philadelphia, became necessary when the oil-polluted Schuylkill could no longer support fishing. The clubhouse stands there today.

Most of the recreational fishing methods employed by the Schuylkill Fishing Company members would not be considered angling in the way that we typically visualize the activity. During a March 1789 meeting of the club, "it was recorded that 'Mr. Benj. Scull, the Prince of Fisherman,' produced a trout, which he this day took in Schuylkill off his lay-out line that measured fifteen inches" (12). Either anchored or drifted in the water, a lay-out line consists of numerous baited hooks attached to smaller lines. The club members also used a plumb line to angle with—"a snood of horsehair, having from three to six small hooks, mounted on a tapering angle rod of twenty to twenty five feet in length." It was noted that an expert angler could take from five to twenty dozen fish using this technique (12).

## New York City Passes the First Angling Law

Generally, people who fished in the eighteenth century were not sport-minded anglers. Like the early members of the Schuylkill Fishing Company, they emphasized the number of fish caught (5). This was the approach likely used at Fresh Water Pond (also known as the Collect) in what is today lower Manhattan in New York City, where the Criminal Court Building now stands (13). In colonial days the pond was a stream-fed, substantial body of water, said to be forty feet deep. It was "famous for its fishing" and "was so popular" that a law was passed by the New York City Common Council in 1734 restricting fishing in the pond to angling (13), no doubt because it was being netted out. When reading the law, which follows, it is not hard to imagine that a city council member with an angling bent may have drafted it. With the passage of this first New York statute related to fishing, the outcome of the battle between the anglers and the "eaters" was starting to look more promising for the fish.

City of
New York

A Law For Preserving The
Fish IN Fresh-Water-Pond

Be it Ordained by the Mayor, Recorder, Aldermen and Assistants of the City of New York, Convened in Common Council and it is hereby Ordained by the Authority of the same, that if any Person or Persons whatsoever do, from henceforth presume to put, place or Cast into the Pond, Commonly Called fresh-Water Pond, belonging to this Corporation, any Hoop-Net, Draw-net, Purse-net, Casting-net, Cod net, Bley-net, or any Other Net or Nets whatsoever, and shall take and Catch any of the fish within the Said Pond, therewith, or by any Other Engine, Machine, Arts, Ways or means whatsoever Other than by Angling, with Angle Rod, Hook and Line only; Every Person so Offending against the Tenour of this Law, shall for Every Offence forfeit and pay the sum of twenty shillings of Current Money of this Colony, to be Recovered before the Mayor, Recorder or any one or more of the Aldermen of the said City, by the Oath of one or more Credible Witnesses, and to be Levied by Distress and sale of the Goods and Chattells of such Offender, the one half thereof to the Informer, and the Other half to the Treasurer of this City for the use of this Corporation, with Reasonable Costs and Charges to be Expended for the Recovery of such forfeiture against the Offender or

Offenders; and for want of sufficient Distress, the Offender or Offenders to be Committed into the Custody of one of the Marshalls of the said City, untill such Offender shall pay such forfeiture with Reasonable Charges of Prosecution as Aforesaid. Dated at the City Hall of the Said City the twenty Eighth day of May in the seventh Year of his Majestys Reign Anno Domini 1734.

By Order of Common Council

Will Sharpas CLERK (14)

## An Early Defense of Fishing

*Angling in America*, written by Charles Eliot Goodspeed, discussed in detail a Christian sermon delivered to a small group of colonists, and quite possibly Native Americans, during the fishing season of 1739. The setting for the homily was a small meetinghouse on the banks of the Merrimack River near Amoskeag Falls in New Hampshire. Published anonymously in 1743 by its author, Joseph Seccombe, in Boston, the sermon does not delve into fishing methods or techniques. Rather, much of it concerns the morality of fishing. We sometimes forget that fishing is a blood sport.

Seccombe began with the Gospel verse of John 21:3, "Simon Peter said to them, 'I am going fishing.'" He then proceeded to develop a defense for fishing along these lines.

> He that takes pleasure in the pains and dying agonies of any lower species of creatures is either a stupid sordid Soul, or a murderer in heart.... But here, in Fishing, we are so far from delighting to see our Fellow-Creature die... we have no more of murderous Tho't [sic] in taking them....
> We are taking something, which God, the
> Creator and Proprietor of all, has given us for Food....
> If I may eat them for Refreshment, I may as well catch them, if this recreate and refresh me. (5)

## Loyalist Anglers

Colonists who had practiced angling in Great Britain or learned it because of their position in American society were often upper-class landed gentry. Usually they were Loyalists, those who supported Great Britain through the Revolutionary period. Two well-known colonial Loyalist anglers were Sir William Johnson and his son Sir John Johnson.

Sir William Johnson

In 1738 young William Johnson emigrated from Ireland and settled in New York's Mohawk Valley to manage an estate purchased by his uncle. There he established a trading post to serve the needs of white settlers and the natives. Surrounded by the Mohawk, one of the Six Nations of the Iroquois, Johnson learned the Mohawk language and dressed in their attire; over time, he gained influence with the Native Americans and created important diplomatic relationships. During the French and Indian Wars, Johnson's sway with the natives proved vital in preventing an Iroquois-French alliance against the British. Fighting beside his son John in 1759 (15), he led nearly one thousand Iroquois warriors as part of the British force to capture Fort Niagara; two months later King George II rewarded him with a baronetcy. The next year, Sir William became British Superintendent of Indian Affairs for the northern colonies, a position that allowed him to amass great wealth and two hundred thousand acres of land on the Mohawk River.

Johnson built his family home, Fort Johnson, in 1749 on the north bank of the Mohawk River. However, sometime prior to 1762, Sir William chose to relocate about nine miles northwest to an area that would afford him greater facility for hunting and fishing (16). To make that possible, he founded Johnson Town (later Johnstown) in 1762, where he built Johnson Hall as his primary family residence.

Johnson Hall, 2015

Also in 1762, Sir William constructed a fishing camp on the south bank of the Sacandaga River (named after a native word signifying "much water") near its confluence with Vlaie Creek, about sixteen miles north of Fort Johnson, a home he still maintained. Once the family had settled in at Johnson Hall, Sir William opened a carriage road from the new mansion to his fishing camp, where he built a comfortable lodge for both hunting and fishing (16). On the roof, he installed a weather vane carved in the shape of a fish (17). Here he pursued "the pleasures of angling, of which he was passionately fond" (18).

Born in 1741 on the bank of the Mohawk River, Sir William's eldest son, John, inherited his father's title, vast lands, and associated fishing waters upon his father's death in 1774. He was subsequently knighted Sir John Johnson and was one of the wealthiest New York colonists (15). However, as result of his allegiance to the king, after the colonists were victorious Sir John abandoned his property and retreated to Canada, where he eventually settled near Montreal. One of the earliest accounts of bass fishing in North America was recorded there. During the summer of 1785, Sir John entertained a traveler named Robert Hunter Jr. In his diary on June 28, Hunter recounted that he had taken a walk after dinner and saw a great number of bass playing in the current. Referring to local anglers, he stated, "They often catch three dozen in the course of half an hour with a fly. I think they are the finest fish I have tasted in America" (19).

Sir John Johnson

# Angling after the Revolutionary War

Following the Revolutionary War, many Loyalists like Sir John abandoned hundreds of thousands of acres of land and abundant waters and returned to England or moved elsewhere. As a result, their angling knowledge retreated with them, and their lands and waters became open to public use by individuals who were largely unaware of the British methods of fishing. Angling practiced after the war carried on as a war casualty. These were tough years; the massive war debt, restriction of exports to Great Britain, a crippled American fleet, and a deluge of British imports that sold for less than comparable American products made life financially difficult (20). Recreational angling was not a priority, and anglers had no money for tackle (10).

Nonetheless, some affluent anglers like George Washington, who "had grown up on the water" (21) and "certainly enjoyed fishing for sport" (21), had the means to continue recreational fishing. For example, when Washington presided over the Constitutional Convention in Philadelphia from May 25 to September 17, 1787, he recorded numerous fishing trips in his diary. The following entry documents a two-day midsummer trip.

> Friday, August 3rd: I went up to Trenton on another Fishing party. Lodged at Colo. Sam Ogdens at the Trenton Works. In the Evening fished, not very successfully.
>
> Saturday, August 4th: In the morning, and between breakfast & dinner, fished again with more success (for perch) than yesterday.

Yet from the viewpoint of ordinary citizens, the possibility of recreational fishing appeared bleak, at least in the East. In contrast, the diverse lands on the western frontier offered seemingly boundless natural resources and new opportunities. The westward migration was about to begin. The Kentucky wilderness appeared to be filled with "bluer" grass and fish-filled waters, a perfect playground for those with an angling bent. Growth and change would continue at a rapid pace for the new country, and angling, originally part of the regional cultures in New England, the Middle Atlantic, Chesapeake, and the Carolinas, would change and grow with it—in Kentucky.

Off for a Fishing Trip, Whitefsh Bay, Ont.
(Courtesy of the Library of Congress)

## Chapter 2

# KENTUCKY, WHERE BLACK BASS FISHING BECAME AN ART

*1775 to 1815*

## Treaty of Sycamore Shoals

The original agricultural system necessary for the colonies to grow, based on existing English farming methods, was unsustainable in the Northeast because much of the land was exhausted by 1800. New England hillsides, lacking fertile soil, were incapable of producing cheap grain like the western lands, and general conditions, especially in the rustic backcountry parts of Virginia and the Carolinas, stimulated a migration from southern farms and villages to the interior frontier. The southerners, hampered by the lack of transportation to coastal markets, also suffered from the unwelcome authority of the Tidewater planters. These conditions and the opportunity for fertile, cheap land provoked migration, without pause, to the western frontier (22).

Just prior to the Revolutionary War, Richard Henderson, a North Carolina judge and land speculator, hired Daniel Boone to assist in negotiations with the Cherokee Nation for the purpose of purchasing land in what is today Kentucky. The parties reached an agreement, known as the Treaty of Sycamore Shoals, in 1775. The terms of the agreement allowed Henderson and his associates to acquire all of the land from the Kentucky River south to the Cumberland River, an area that covers much of the present commonwealth of Kentucky and some of what is now Tennessee. There were British colonial legal issues surrounding the agreement, but because the deal occurred at a most fortuitous time —the beginning of the Revolutionary War—the agreement stood, and the Kentucky lands became available for settlement by citizens of the new country (23).

In the ten years following 1790, the population of Kentucky exploded, increasing by 200 percent (24). To those wanting to escape the crowded cities in the East, Kentucky offered plentiful new land, rich soil, and freedom of opportunity that made it a paradise for those settling there. The especially desirable Bluegrass region of the state featured not only rolling hills, fertile soil, and pastures, but plentiful rivers and streams that provided the perfect environment for angling to thrive.

# Kentucky Waters

Kentucky's initial settlers were undoubtedly amazed at the many miles of rivers and streams they found there. A study of water transportation corridors commissioned by the Commonwealth of Kentucky Transportation Cabinet in February 2000 noted that Kentucky has 49,100 navigable (canoe-floatable) miles of rivers, streams, and tributaries (25), more than any state except Alaska (26). Additionally, the study identified 40,900 unnavigable miles, for a whopping total of 90,000 linear miles of water (27). Of those, 62,000 miles are fishable streams—a truly staggering figure. In that water are 244 species of native freshwater fish, surpassed only by Tennessee and Alabama (27).

Ninety-five percent of the early Kentucky settlers migrated from the colonies of Virginia, North Carolina, and Maryland. Almost all were of British stock, and probably more than half originally came from Scotland or the north of England (28). Hailing from these areas of the British Isles, many had no doubt developed prowess in casting the fly for trout and salmon. Their love of fishing was practically inborn. These devoted anglers were familiar with the writings of Walton and others; surely some had retained their tackle or that of their forebears. Many were educated, astute individuals who yearned to indulge their piscatorial hobby. What they soon discovered, however, was that the familiar fish species abundant in their homeland were absent from Kentucky waters. Instead, the magnificent streams and rivers were filled with smallmouth bass, walleye, and muskellunge, presenting different opportunities and challenges for their entertainment.

Abundant among the native fish inhabiting these waters was the black bass—specifically, the smallmouth version of the species, *Micropterus dolomieu*, a fish described by Dr. James Alexander Henshall as "inch for inch and pound for pound, the gamest fish that swims" (29). Henshall, born in Baltimore on February 29, 1836, and known as "The Apostle of the Black Bass" (30), anointed Kentucky as the place where black bass fishing became an art. A physician, prolific angling author, and fish culturist, his most famous literary work—*Book of the Black Bass*, published in 1881—is an all-time classic. In the forty-seven years since 1970, the year the Bass Anglers Sportsman's Society started reproducing Henshall's book, hundreds of thousands of copies have been disseminated across the globe.

## Early Kentucky Anglers

During the Civil War, Dr. Henshall served as a physician in Cynthiana, Kentucky. There he became intimately familiar with the area, the resident anglers, and the history of angling in the Bluegrass region. Consequently, he provided valuable insight into the customs of early anglers who settled this region: "The good people of the blue-grass region of Kentucky exhibit many of the distinctive traits and customs of their English and Scotch-Irish ancestors; but in no feature is this heredity more pronounced than in their love for angling. With them angling is... in no sense a fad or hobby" (3). It should be no surprise that the new immigrants to Kentucky, determined to continue their beloved pastime, had quickly evaluated the Kentucky angling environment: the fish species and the approach necessary to catch them.

Kentuckians soon realized that bass are insatiable eaters. Based on examinations of stomach contents, fishery biologists agree that bass will eat whatever prey is available; if they can get their mouths around it and inhale it, they eat it. Most individuals have seen large freshwater aquariums (approximately four hundred to five hundred gallons, somewhat smaller than those featured in the sporting and fishing superstores); what many have not witnessed is feeding time. A restaurant in northern Minnesota has a very large aquarium full of middling-size largemouth. Watching them feed is astounding. A two-gallon bucket crammed full of large live minnows is dumped into the tank, and the feeding frenzy is immediate and intense. The aquarium occupants suck in everything in sight within the first thirty seconds and poke around for another half minute, picking up the lingering few. Bass eat crayfish, frogs, lizards, snakes, other fish, and even small birds; trophy-size bass will eat other fish ten to twelve inches long (31).

Understanding the nature of their voracious prey, the immigrants next considered the method they had to use to catch bass. The sport-minded anglers intended to use the existing familiar tackle, but this soon presented a significant and unexpected problem: the streams were too deep to wade in order to fly-cast. Worse yet, the waters that the fish haunted were far from shore and well beyond the casting reach of fly-fishers.

Having an inventive nature, these early Kentuckians began to employ live bait and the technique of still-fishing to catch bass. A favorite bait was "the steel-backed minnow... which is a very common minnow, brassy in coloration, and much mottled with dark blotches; it has thick, tough lips, almost sucker like" (32).

The simplest of angling methods, still-fishing can be very successful assuming there are fish in the vicinity. If not, the bait must be moved to water that is more fertile. A long pole, or rod, with a length of line tied to the end is effective for moving bait, but only to the extent that it is long enough to reach the desired area. In Kentucky, giant cane, a native plant used for numerous purposes by Native Americans, was available for making angling rods. In southern states, historical accounts report cane growing "as high as a man on horse-back could reach with an umbrella" (33). However, even these cane rods proved too short to reach the distant fish; a better solution was required.

Adding a fishing reel would aid in moving bait. Two types of single-action reels were available at the time: the English reel, made of brass, and the homemade reel. Homemade types typically consisted of a wooden sewing spool mounted within a frame that spun on an axle when a crank handle on the side was turned. On either reel, the handle and spool rotated at the same speed. Simply mounting such a reel on a cane rod would make it possible to move the bait farther. However, it would have been difficult to make a cast of more than a few feet, because the inertia generated by the single-action reel spool was too much for the weight of the bait to overcome. Consequently, casting required stripping sufficient line off the spool and coiling it on the ground prior to making a cast.

## A New Type of Fishing Reel

The pressing issue for early Kentucky anglers became how to present a baited hook across a larger area of water to increase the chances of a catch. The answer was that a new type of fishing reel was required—a reel that permitted casting from the line spool so that the weight of the bait tossed by the rod would pull the line off the spool. The distance that the bait could be cast would depend on the bait's weight and the free-running attributes of the reel. Therefore a geared, multiplying reel, where one turn of the reel crank handle equals multiple turns of the reel spool, was required (34).

Multiplying reels use gears to rotate the spool more rapidly than the crank that turns it. In these types of reels, a spool mounted within a frame spins on an axle, one side of which is inserted through a small pinion gear. A larger drive gear, connected to the crank handle, meshes with the pinion gear in order to rotate the spool more rapidly than the crank. Such reels were available in England as early as the 1760s (35), and some found their way to America during the same period (36); but at best they must have been uncommon to most Kentucky anglers. However, according to Frank M. Stewart III, a multiplying reel marked "O. Ustonson, Maker to His Majesty Temple Bar London" was discovered "in a town near the Kentucky River within 60 miles of Paris, Kentucky" and passed down, generation to generation, within the same local family for over a hundred

years. Stewart tells us that the exact history of the reel is unknown, but that it probably dates to the early 1800s, prior to 1839 (37).

To produce a comparable or even better reel would take a first-class artisan competent in precision engineering and machining. Nineteenth-century artisans with that competency had a common skill set: performing precision work on a lathe and gear-cutting machine to construct small metal parts such as gears, springs, threaded screws, and balance wheels, and fitting, finishing, and assembling those parts into a final product.

Among those who were talented and trained in these skills were gunsmiths. When the frontier began to open up, the demand for firearms increased. Gunsmiths migrated westward to make and repair the long-barreled Kentucky rifles made famous by the early frontiersmen (such as one who helped found Kentucky, Daniel Boone). As each area settled down and became civilized, the gun trade slacked off, so the gunsmiths sought other trades. Some worked as watchmakers, silversmiths, and jewelers between their gunsmithing jobs, until gradually these trades predominated (38).

## George Snyder: The First Kentucky Reel Maker

George Snyder, a silversmith and watchmaker, was one such artisan. Born in Bucks, Pennsylvania, circa 1781, Snyder moved to Paris, Kentucky, in the early 1800s. An ardent angler and president of the Bourbon County Angling Club in 1810 (34), he was clearly acquainted with other anglers in the area. Henshall wrote that "a few anglers were fly-fishers, but most of them were bait fishers" (39) and that "these anglers were among the best and brightest and most intelligent and cultivated men of that period, who adorned the several professions or were the lordly proprietors of vast domains of perennial green" (40). Snyder knew that a multiplying reel was required. Although it's a remote possibility, he may have even examined one, such as the English Ustonson model discovered much later within sixty miles of his home.

Some Kentuckians, familiar with the celebrated anglers of the Clay families in Bourbon County, believed that one of the Clays might have initially persuaded Snyder to make such a reel. Whether or not that is true, Snyder did make one around 1815 (41). Consequently, for many years following, most individuals believed that Snyder invented the multiplying reel (42). This misconception, which arose due to the lack of common knowledge surrounding early British multiplying reels, is no longer widely held.

Most now consider him to have invented the "art" of reel making by applying precision design and machining concepts to the process (36).

Thus the history of the American baitcasting reel began in the Bluegrass region of Kentucky when George Snyder produced the first American-refined version of a multiplying reel. Snyder made a relatively small number of these reels. After his death in 1841, his two sons, John and Charles Snyder, produced a few more prior to 1844 (34). When Steven K. Vernon and Frank M. Stewart III published their watershed book *Fishing Reel Makers of Kentucky* in 1992, they documented nine Snyder reels. In 1995 Ray Carver discovered a small brass Snyder reel at a Michigan antique market. Known to collectors as the Carver Snyder Reel, it was dated to circa 1815 or possibly earlier by a group of antique reel experts. At this writing, only these ten Snyder reels are known to exist.

During Snyder's lifetime, mass production did not exist; he produced handmade reels. The demand for the new "Kentucky reel" (those reels produced following Snyder's archetype), driven by the huge numbers of black bass, walleye, pike, and muskellunge that populated Bluegrass waters, far outstripped the possible supply of reels. Even in the peak days of Kentucky reel production, according to a famed artisan of the time, three reel makers working full-time may have been able to produce only seven reels a month (43), assuming the proper equipment and tooling were available. Additionally, anglers who could reasonably pay the high price for such a reel were few, especially in the earliest days.

Large Snyder reel

(Photograph courtesy of Gene Burch
Photography, Frankfort, KY)

According to George Snyder's grandson, R. J. Snyder, the large reel is one of the earliest made by his grandfather. Originally used for muskellunge, pike and walleye fishing, the end plates of this brass reel measure 2 3/8 inches in diameter. The length of the line spool as noted by Henshall also measured 2 3/8 inches (34). Other historians have reported the spool length to be 2 5/16 inches (45).

When Snyder made the first Kentucky reels, a routine business practice was that "customers didn't ask the price... they ordered and were charged what the artisan thought it was worth" (44). I am unaware of Snyder's business practices or whether he made reels as a business or as a hobby. Another reel maker who followed Snyder by fifteen years, Theodore Noel, seems to have done the latter. Noel, a maker of watches and clocks in Frankfort, made reels for "personal gratification and to supply the needs of those friends whose pastime was angling" (38). He apparently used a Snyder reel as a design model. Unfortunately, the whereabouts of any Noel reels, if still in existence, are a mystery. Most historians and collectors believe that he made a small quantity, because none are available for examination. Consequently, it cannot be determined whether Noel replicated Snyder's design, improved upon it, or possibly did an inadequate job of copying it. Further, it remains unknown whether succeeding reel makers followed Snyder's design or Noel's.

The high cost of the reel, along with its intrinsic value based on the pleasure that it added to the angling game, immediately made the reel an object of veneration. Handmade reels remained in a rarified atmosphere, not only during the days when they actually functioned as angling tools but also in later years. They have been handed down from generation to generation to become part of the angling paraphernalia lovingly assembled into collections by twenty-first-century enthusiasts. The exquisitely crafted Kentucky reel represents the defining moment in the evolution of the fishing reel, and it holds a coveted place above all others in the mystique of the sport.

The metamorphosis of the angling method from still-fishing to baitcasting began with the manufacture of Snyder's first reel. It lasted until about 1881. The history of the angling transformation in Kentucky and the evolution of the American baitcasting reel, tied together at the hip, are fundamental to understanding the development of the sport. The following chapter will explore the history of the artisans who produced the Kentucky reel. George Snyder was only the first in a long line of esteemed Kentucky reel makers.

A Veteran Angler

(Courtesy of the Library of Congress)

# Chapter 3
# THE KENTUCKY BAITCASTING REEL

*Mid-1830s to 1928*

## J. L. Sage Helps Illuminate the History

James L. (J. L.) Sage, one of the lesser-known Kentucky reel makers and longtime friend of Dr. James Henshall, held a unique position with respect to the other Kentucky artisans making reels. Sage lived around the corner; he was part of the same crowd. He was not a bashful man; Sage spoke his mind. Certain episodes and personal relationships in Sage's life uniquely position him to illuminate events in the story of the baitcasting reel that otherwise would have remained unknown or unappreciated. His intricate knowledge of the Kentucky reel as both a maker and an angler, along with his keen personal observations of those who produced it, provide deep insights into parts of the account that otherwise would have remained thirsty.

The 1850 census of Franklin County, Kentucky, recorded that James L. Sage, age twenty-eight, was born in Hartford, Connecticut. Initially he apprenticed as a gunsmith and maker of fine mathematical instruments, working those trades in Frankfort, Kentucky. According to Henshall, Sage repaired reels in Frankfort as early as 1842, when he was twenty years old. Using the tools with which he made Morse telegraph instruments, Sage constructed his first fishing reel in 1848. Henshall said it was the smallest reel he had ever seen; Sage used it to fly-cast for bass.

In about 1850, Sage obtained a job at Frankfort's gas and water works doing "rough work" such as pipe fitting. In 1853 he relocated to the town of Paris in Bourbon County, Kentucky. There Mr. Jeffery, the individual responsible for constructing the town's public works, employed him through the end of the Civil War. In 1865 Sage returned to Frankfort, where he worked as a United States gauger, testing gas and water operations and regulating flows into pipelines. In 1883 he finally began making fishing reels full-time, patterning them after the type initially produced by Jacob Hardman, a Louisville reel maker (41).

Sage resided at 234 St. Clair in Frankfort, near the old First Baptist church. The business section of the 1884–85 Frankfort directory lists J. L. Sage under "Fishing Reel Manufacturers," and the residence section notes the same address for his home. There Sage produced at least ninety-nine reels, since one of them, apparently made just before he left Frankfort in 1885, is marked with serial number "99" (45).

In 1885 Sage relocated to Lexington. The 1887 Lexington city directory lists him under "Manufacturer—Fishing Reels" and shows him residing at 21½ W. Main Street. In 1896 he moved to 137 East Main in Lexington. During his time in Lexington, he produced approximately 225 more reels.

Sage purchased a burial plot in Section J of the Frankfort Cemetery in 1888, and on September 8, 1900, he was interred there (46).

## The Meek Brothers

Jonathan Fleming (J. F.) Meek (34), born in Virginia in about 1812 (45), lived in Danville, Kentucky, throughout his childhood days. He reportedly worked there as an apprentice silversmith to a Samuel Ayres (41). However, in order for this to be true, his apprenticeship would had to have been when J. F. Meek was about twelve years old, because Samuel Ayers died in Danville on September 16, 1824 (47). It would seem more likely that J. F. Meek was an apprentice to Samuel Ayres's son, Thomas Robinson Jameson Ayres, who was born on November 28, 1805, in Danville (47). The younger Ayres was a silversmith, gunsmith, and jeweler in Danville from 1823 to 1857 (48), sharing a building there with his brother Samuel, a dentist (47).

In the early 1830s, J. F. Meek moved to Frankfort, Kentucky, about forty miles north of Danville (45), to engage in the jewelry and watchmaking trade. According to Sage, "Meek was a fisher himself, and loved the sport" (41). He became associated with Mason Brown, a longtime resident and angler. Sage claims that Brown and J. F. Meek "used to go out hunting and fishing together a great deal" (41). Brown, subsequently appointed as a judge on the Kentucky Circuit bench in 1939, was the son of John Brown, aide-de-camp to Lafayette and the first senator from Kentucky.

J. F. Meek's younger brother, Benjamin Franklin (B. F.) Meek, was born on September 15, 1816, in a section of Mercer County, Kentucky, that is now part of Boyle County. Although he lived near the Salt River, the younger Meek cared little for the sport of angling because he admittedly had little patience to wait for fish to bite. Perhaps this intolerance was known by others, because in a small town like 1830s Danville, everyone knew everyone. For this reason, J. F. Meek may have vouched for his younger brother when he too pursued an apprenticeship with Ayres.

As reported by Sage, "Ben was a prodigal son, and went wild" as a youth (41). Regardless, B. F. Meek, "a better mechanic at fifteen than most men who thought they were good mechanics ever got to be" (38), secured the job as apprentice. Sometime after his training with Ayers, he moved to Frankfort to work with his older brother.

In the early spring of 1835, when both brothers were working in J. F. Meek's Frankfort watch shop, Mason Brown came in to have a reel repaired. Then he decided that instead of a repair, he required a new reel. He prevailed on his friend J. F. to make him one. J. F. Meek had not yet made a reel, but perhaps because he had the judge's old one as a model, he consented to try it.

There was one problem: the only gear-cutting machine in Kentucky was located forty miles south in Danville. J. F. Meek made the trip—but how? The recently completed rail line ran only to Lexington, and a horseback trip would take a long time. Still, there were other reasonable alternatives of traveling by boat, carriage, or both.

J. F. Meek made the eighty-mile round trip to Danville, produced the gear wheels, and finished the reel back in Frankfort with his watch tools (41). Finally he presented Brown with the reel. Word spread that Brown's "soul was filled with joy" over the new reel, and afterward, his fishing creel was filled with the "speckled beauties of Elkhorn Creek." The judge wasted no time informing his friends and neighbors of how pleased he was with J. F. Meek's product. Later, when bragging about the reel, he was reported to have intoned, "The Meek shall inherit the earth," since one of that family had furnished him with the means of taking the "treasures of the waters" (49).

J. L. Sage also held the judge's new reel in high regard, remarking that it was very small and long, like Snyder's reel, and was "a mighty good one, a better one than Snyder made" (41). Henshall described Snyder's archetype reel that Meek probably used as his example: "All of the Snyder reels... are quite narrow in diameter of the spool, and also much longer than those in the present day. This is in accordance with the fact that a long narrow spool runs more rapidly... than where the spool is short and of greater diameter" (34).

## B. C. Milam's Apprenticeship

In 1835 Benjamin Cave (B. C.) Milam, age fourteen, went to Frankfort, Kentucky, and became a watchmaking apprentice to Beverly Noel, whose brother Theodore had previously produced at least one multiplying reel around 1830. It is apparent that B. C. Milam was familiar with the early efforts to make Kentucky reels, because in 1836 he visited Paris, Kentucky, and saw Snyder's reels (34). In 1837 Noel quit business, and B. C. Milam became an apprentice to J. F. Meek (50).

It may be that Milam's new apprenticeship position originated because of the increase in work driven by Brown's endorsement of the new reel. The extra business spurred the Meek brothers to build an addition to the store "for the sole purpose of making reels" (49). The small Frankfort shop, apparently an initial success, identified these early reels by stamping them with the trade name "Meek" (45); this trademark quickly changed to "J.F. & B.F. Meek," thus reflecting the new partner status of the two brothers.

The Meeks' new partnership may have experienced some challenges early on. In Frankfort on December 8, 1840, the brothers sent a letter along with a thirty-dollar payment to an individual with the surname of Fletcher to pay off a personal note. The letter indicated that had it not been for the "unavoidable circumstances" Fletcher was already aware of, the Meek brothers would have sent the payment sooner. Additionally, the brothers owed Fletcher more money on a second note that they promised to pay off in January 1841. The letter was signed J. F. and B. F. Meek (51).

Around this same time, J. F. Meek divided the shop's workload: he assigned his brother the reel making, while he performed the watch work. Perhaps related to the challenge of accruing the money to pay Fletcher back, B. F. Meek spent a year as a traveling watch and clock repairer sometime after 1837 (45), a hiatus no doubt made possible by Milam's presence in the business as a new apprentice.

## Damming the Kentucky River

Immediately prior to Milam's apprenticeship in 1836, the town of Frankfort was full of activity. The Commonwealth had begun building locks and dams on the Kentucky River to provide reliable year-round navigation from the river's mouth to its interior sources, thus allowing barges to reach Kentucky's lumber- and coal-rich eastern region. By 1842, after many trials, tribulations, and financial woes, five of the state's locks and dams planned on the Kentucky River were completed, and approximately half the river's length accommodated slack-water navigation. The steamboat packet *Ocean* became the first vessel to steam upriver, pass through Locks 1 through 4, and navigate the completed project to Frankfort (52).

The nineteenth-century development of the Mississippi River and its tributaries allowed the large-scale transport of passengers and freight, and the volume of traffic was significant. Steamboats from Pittsburgh, Cincinnati, and Louisville that traveled up and down the Ohio River could now also navigate the Kentucky River and steam on to Frankfort. The river ports were full of activity: from 1838 to 1852, the number of boats docked at Cincinnati rose from five hundred to an all-time record of eight thousand (53). Sage said that at Frankfort in 1843, "boats used to lie up at a lock, and the passengers would get out and go fishing" using reels made by a Louisville man named Hardman, who "made a 3 bar reel, shorter by one third than the old Sneider [*sic*] model" (41).

Paddle steamer 'Evansville of Evansville' Rear-wheel type paddlesteamer that worked the Ohio River. Indiana, USA. 1887."

(Clarence O. Becker Archive / Alamy Stock Photo)

## Hardman, a Louisville Reel Maker

Sage stated that because B. F. Meek observed the Hardman reels used by the steamboat passengers, he immediately began incorporating the same improvements into his new reels. In his *Book of the Black Bass*, James Henshall discussed and provided drawings of Hardman's enhancements.

About the year 1843 a very fine workman and expert watchmaker, of Louisville, Ky., named J. W. Hardman, began making multiplying reelsa... a great improvement on those previously made by others. He shortened the spool and increased the diameter, affixed the pillars to the diskplates by screws instead of riveting, added some ornamentation, and altogether made the first true and substantial improvements in the "Kentucky reel," both as to its practicability and appearance, and these were followed thereafter by all other makers.... The Hardman reel illustrated is the property of Mr. J. F. Speed.... It was made about 1845, and is a very handsome piece of work, of German silver (34).

FIG. 3i.
Hardman Reel.

FIG. 32.
Hardman Reel Gearing.

Illustrations of Hardman's reel from *Book of the Black Bass*

Henshall went on to say:

> An old reel stamped "Meek & Milam" was exhibited in my collection, made somewhere about 1844, and is shown in the accompanying illustrations.... With the exception of the ornamental bars or pillars of the Hardman reel, this reel is a close imitation of it in its general form, in the sliding buttons and their screws, in the collar and the retaining screw of the crank (34).

The upshot of Henshall's statements is that Hardman's improvements to the reel preceded those of the Meek brothers. Regarding his own reels, Sage stated that he too "followed the old Hardman type in general form" to produce reels.

Since Henshall's time, a number of historians remained somewhat reluctant to endorse the allegation that Hardman's improvements to the reel preceded those made by Meek. The primary apprehension appears to have been a lack of public evidence that Hardman was in the Louisville vicinity during 1843–45, when Henshall and Sage indicate that the reels were built. Previously, the earliest that Hardman could be placed in the Louisville area was 1866–67. However, information that is now available shows that J. W. Hardman was in the area much earlier.

Jacob Wolf Hardman was born to John D. and Elizabeth (Waggoner) Hardman on January 2, 1801, at Little Skin Creek, Lewis County, Virginia (now West Virginia). On February 4, 1829, in Washington County, Indiana—approximately twenty miles northwest of Louisville—Hardman married Moriah Rodman (born July 6, 1806) in a ceremony officiated by Ebenezer Patrick, a county judge. The 1830 census lists Jacob W. Hardman residing in Washington County as head of household with a female between twenty and thirty years old and a male child under the age of five, evidently his wife Moriah and a newborn. The 1840 census lists Jacob Hardman as residing in the Ohio River port town of Madison, Indiana, about forty miles upriver from Louisville. By 1860 the census indicates that J. W. Hardman resided in Louisville, Jefferson County, Kentucky, and worked as a watchmaker. Hardman died on April 25, 1876, in Louisville and was interred directly across the river in the Eastern Cemetery of Jeffersonville, Indiana. I have seen it noted, but was unable to confirm, that Hardman's wife, Moriah, died in Louisville in October 1874.

Collectors consider Hardman a minor reel maker because they are aware of only three surviving Hardman reels, and one of those is unmarked (45). Since Hardman's reels were held in such high regard technically by both Henshall and Sage, I have wondered why Hardman did not produce more reels. An inventor, silversmith, artisan, and watchmaker, Hardman possessed a surname that possibly forewarned others of his confrontational disposition. Sage referred to him as "cranky" and also said that if Hardman "happened to take a new notion, he would drop his work and everything else, and sit and study; then when he got a thing half worked out, as like it or not he would throw it away and never finish it" (41). In the same vein, Jonathan Meek, in an 1861 letter to B. C. Milam, said that Hardman "is certainly the most disagreeable man to have any business with that I have anything to do with" (45).

Conjecture may have Hardman just fatigued of making reels, or his unique personality may have driven customers away. Regardless, the small number of reels he produced does not diminish his contributions. Hardman was in the right locale at the right time in history, and he possessed the expertise and the means to have produced the reels used by the steamboat passengers in 1843, just as Sage claims. Two of our earliest Kentucky reel historians, Henshall and Sage, respected Hardman's talent and paid tribute to his contributions, Now, a more generous recognition of Hardman as the first known reel maker in the Louisville area seems appropriate.

## B. F. Meek and B. C. Milam

In 1846 B. C. Milam left the reel-making business for a short time and volunteered for service in the Mexican-American War as a cavalry captain. Frank M. Stewart, reel historian and author, wrote, "I believe that there is a strong possibility that Sage learned reel making in the 'JF&BF' Meek shop in Frankfort, possibly when the principal reel maker, B. C. Milam, was away during the war with Mexico in 1846–47" (54). After his return from the war in 1847, Milam became a partner in the Meeks' business (circa 1849). As a result, the firm's name changed from "J. F. & B. F. Meek" to "J. F. Meek & Co," but the maker's mark remained unchanged. In 1852 this business failed (34). B. F. Meek and B. C. Milam formed a new partnership in early 1853. In that arrangement, Milam assumed responsibility for reel making and Meek for jewelry and watchmaking. The trademark used for the previous fifteen years, "J. F. & B. F. Meek," now changed to read "Meek & Milam." This partnership ended in 1855, with Milam keeping the rights to use the Meek & Milam trade name.

Although no longer partners, both men continued doing business at the same Frankfort address, with B. F. Meek making watches and jewelry on the building's first floor and Milam making reels and clocks on the second. Milam preferred making reels to watches, and that probably kept the reel business growing. Nevertheless, Sage put a slightly different twist on it: during an interview he said, "In the new firm Meek made the reels and Milam made the watches, but Milam made poor watches, so they traded work, and Milam made the reels" (41). The men would share the same Frankfort location through the Civil War years and beyond. During this time (1855–1880), Milam produced 100 percent of the reels. His son, John W. Milam, born July 12, 1859, became a reel-making apprentice in his father's shop in 1876 at the age of seventeen.

By 1881, when B. C. Milam became aware that B. F. Meek would be moving to Louisville to start a new business, he stopped using the "Meek & Milam, Frankfort, KY" maker stamp on the reels and began stamping them with his own mark, "B. C. Milam, Frankfort, KY" (55). In 1883 B. C. Milam also began adding serial numbers to his reels. When Vernon and Stewart published *Fishing Reel Makers of Kentucky* in 1992, they noted that 5171 was the lowest known serial number, which suggested to them that B. C. Milam began with the number 5000. Milam continued using the "B. C. Milam" stamp on new reels until 1896, approximately six years after John Milam became a partner.

A new reel stamp was created in 1896, but it did not reference John as a partner with "& Son." Rather, the mark was "B. C. Milam" in a straight line, with the phrase "The Frankfort Kentucky Reel"—a term he had been using in his advertising for the previous four years—added in an arch above the name (55). By now this reel had become globally famous, taking international first prize medals at the World's Columbian Exposition in Chicago in 1893; the International Fisheries Exposition in Bergen, Norway, in 1898; the Exposition Universelle in Paris, France, in 1900; and the Louisiana Purchase Exposition in 1904.

Mr. Benjamin F. Meek.

B. F. Meek

Mr. Benjamin C. Milam.

B. C. Milam

(From *Book of the Black Bass*)

Following B. F. Meek's 1882 reentry into the reel-making business in Louisville, he stamped the new reels with a "B. F. Meek, Louisville, KY" maker's mark. By around 1890 two of Meek's sons, Pitman and Sylvanus, had entered the business, and the firm's name changed to "B. F. Meek & Sons." However, the "B. F. Meek, Louisville, KY" stamp remained on the reels until circa 1896–97, when it was changed to "B. F. Meek & Sons."

B. F. Meek No. 3 reel (mid-1880s)

B. F. Meek retired in 1898 and sold the company to a corporation that operated it under the name "B.F. Meek & Sons, Inc." With few exceptions, the era of handmade fishing reels was now over. B. F. Meek died on June 23, 1901, in Frankfort, Kentucky.

## False Advertising

In 1901, a few years following the sale of Meek's Louisville business, the new corporate owners became defendants in a false advertising case in which B. C. and John Milam were the plaintiffs. Following are some excerpts from the opinion rendered by Judge Shackelford Miller regarding the controversy.

> The plaintiffs, B. C. Milam & Son, now complain that the defendant corporation B. F. Meek & Sons, with the design and purpose to get plaintiff's trade and to deceive the public is now and has since its purchase from Ben F. Meek in 1898, been manufacturing reels in Louisville which it puts on the market advertised as the original "Frankfort, Kentucky Reel."... To allow the defendant corporation to reap the benefit of the plaintiff's long and honorable course in business indirectly naming or

calling its reel made in Louisville as the Frankfort Reel
or the Frankfort, Kentucky Reel... would be in violation of
the broad and equitable rule of fair trade laid down in the
many authorities above cited.

Judge Miller rendered his opinion on November 14, 1901, ruling in favor
of B. C. and John Milam (55). The defendants made an appeal, which was
dismissed. On November 14, 1902, they were ordered to pay the Milams
$29.26 for court costs (45), about the cost of a Milam reel at the time.

A short time later, the Milam reel stamp was changed to read "B.C.
Milam & Son, Frankfort, KY." Their reels remained produced by hand,
even though others had succumbed to mechanization.

## The End of an Era

B. C. Milam died in Frankfort on January 29, 1904, and was interred in
the cemetery there. An obituary published in *Forest and Stream* magazine
elegized, "Captain Benjamin Cave Milam, died at his home in Frankfort,
Ky., on Friday afternoon last, after rounding out the period of a full-orbed
life, at the age of 82, profoundly lamented by all who knew him. Preceded
by Daly, Meek, Sage, and Gayle, he was the last of the Kentucky line of
inventors and makers of hand-made fishing reels to answer the summons
to cross the Great Divide."

John Milam making reels in Frankfort

(Courtesy of the Kentucky Historical Society)

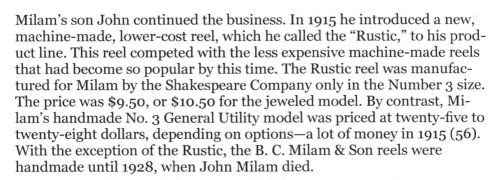

Milam's son John continued the business. In 1915 he introduced a new, machine-made, lower-cost reel, which he called the "Rustic," to his product line. This reel competed with the less expensive machine-made reels that had become so popular by this time. The Rustic reel was manufactured for Milam by the Shakespeare Company only in the Number 3 size. The price was $9.50, or $10.50 for the jeweled model. By contrast, Milam's handmade No. 3 General Utility model was priced at twenty-five to twenty-eight dollars, depending on options—a lot of money in 1915 (56). With the exception of the Rustic, the B. C. Milam & Son reels were handmade until 1928, when John Milam died.

J. L. Sage has had plenty to say about the history of the Kentucky reel. Who is more fitting to close this chapter?

> A good many people... have the idea that the Kentucky
> reel is the product of one man, or at the most the product
> of two firms, and that there is a patent covering a certain
> definite form of it. That is not the case. There are several
> parties who have made or are making the Kentucky reel,
> and these reels are nearly as good, one as another. This
> type was established long ago, and there has not been
> so much change in it as you might think (41).

J. L. Sage

(From *Book of the Black Bass*)

# Chapter 4

# INDUSTRIALIZATION IN AMERICA

*1793 to 1893*

## Where Have All the Salmon Gone?

During the same period in which Kentuckians were working to refine the new multiplying reels, the US population was accelerating at an unimaginable rate. According to the 1800 census, the US population was 5,308,483 souls. Ten years later, it had increased by 36.4 percent. As a result, food production in the country had to ramp up to match that growth. Massive amounts of timber had been cleared for new farms in the Northeast, transforming the forests into a checkerboard of tilled land separated by fences, random ponds, and treed areas. Inevitably, land erosion began to take hold, and watershed wildlife habitats began to deteriorate.

Parallel with the growing population, America was industrializing. The Slater textile mill, built in 1793 on the Blackstone River in Pawtucket, Rhode Island, became the first factory in the country (57). Subsequent factories would also be built near rivers and fast-moving streams, not only for cheap transportation of goods but so that direct-drive waterwheels could be mounted underneath the structures to power the production machinery (58). Industrialization was destined to be nourished by water. Dams and canals built to divert water to industrial mills in the city were not a good omen for the fish habitat.

Left, first US factory, Slater's Mill; Right, a Slater power turbine.

(Courtesy of the Library of Congress)

That first textile mill marked the birth of the Industrial Revolution. It also marked the beginning of the transition of Narragansett Bay into an industrial outhouse. Within a few short decades, Rhode Island became the nation's most industrialized state: wool and cotton factories were amassed along the Blackstone River, with the town of Pawtucket single-handedly supporting twenty-nine cotton mills (59). The river became a dumping ground for industrial waste and raw sewage from the ever-increasing population; polluted runoff would soon be found in the ponds and lakes. Growth and change, both good and bad, continued at a rapid pace. In less than two decades (1793–1810), the workers employed by factories in the Northeast grew from zero to over 2.5 percent of the workforce employed in the entire country (60).

What was the impact of the population growth and Industrial Revolution on the fish? Land erosion, dam construction on the mainstream rivers and tributaries, and pollution caused by both industries and individuals became insurmountable obstacles to the riparian wildlife and fish populations. The dams were impassable for the Atlantic salmon and American eel, fish that required unobstructed access both downstream and upstream for migration, spawning, and feeding. Salmon had disappeared from the rivers, and by 1850 eels were locally decimated in many watersheds (61). As a result, angling, netting, and clubbing methods of fish harvest were no longer performed in those places. The effects of population and industrial explosion were intensely concentrated in the cities, where overcrowding, lack of sewage systems, and contaminated drinking water made life risky. The often ugly process of fundamentally altering America from a rural society to an urban industrial society had irrevocably begun.

## "The Great Leap Westward" (62)

While the fish population was ravaged in many parts of the Northeast, awareness of recreational fishing ignited in Kentucky. The nation's expansion, which Teddy Roosevelt liked to refer to as the great leap westward, was highly dependent on water. Beyond its ability to support the fish habitat and power the new industrial base, water was a primary mode of transportation and fundamental to the success of the new nation. Unimpeded use of the Mississippi River without interference from Spain or France was crucial for America's security, movement of goods, and westward expansion. The Louisiana Purchase, a vast area of land bought from France in 1803, not only secured the Mississippi but also added 530 million acres of territory. The newly opened lands were settled and developed rapidly. By 1820, one-fifth of America's ten million people lived west of the Appalachians (63).

The United States purchased Florida and the Oregon Territory from Spain in 1819. Then, because of the Mexican-American War (1846–48), Mexico in 1848 was forced to relinquish the region of North America known today as the southwestern United States. Within two years of the 1849 Gold Rush, the population in California jumped from eight hundred people to one hundred thousand (64). The country had now expanded across the entire continent.

## A Well-Respected Man

During the Mexican-American War, a captivating slice of historical lore related to angling occurred. It had nothing to do with fishing, but rather reflected on the character of one of the central figures in early angling history, B. C. Milam.

As related in Chapter 3, in 1846 B. C. Milam left the reel-making business for a short time and volunteered for service in the Mexican-American War. He was the captain of Company C of the First Regiment Kentucky Cavalry, commanded by Col. Humphrey Marshall. During the battle of Buena Vista, Milam's company lost three mounted troops. Due to the war's immediate and pressing circumstances, he buried them in Mexico. Upon his return home, Milam helped convince the Frankfort Trustees and County Court to appropriate money for him to return to Mexico and recover the bodies of his slain brothers-in-arms. Milam returned to Mexico, exhumed the remains of his companions, and escorted them home for burial with honors in the Kentucky State Cemetery at Frankfort.

While that information is verifiable history, the following is highly feasible lore. While recruiting solders in Frankfort, Captain Milam rejected an underage boy's enlistment. The boy later reappeared with his mother, who pleaded with Milam to accept her son; and so he did. During the campaign at the Battle of Buena Vista, Milam, who had been ordered to execute a cavalry charge against the vaunted Mexican Lancers, told the boy to forgo the charge. The boy did not obey, but took to his mount and made the charge against orders. When the battle ended, he was found pierced by a lance, killed in action. The boy's body, subsequently returned to Frankfort with other Ken-

War Memorial on the Frankfort Cemetery State Mound.

tuckians killed in the battle, was somehow left unidentified. Consequently, the grave of the young boy remained unmarked and overlooked for many years. It is said that because no one knew his name, he lies there today within the State Mound area of the cemetery in an unmarked grave. Some Frankfort residents informally consider the grave as the resting place of the Unknown Soldier (65).

Kentucky's heroes of the Mexican-American War are interred in the State Mound area of the Kentucky State Cemetery, one of the most handsome and dignified memorials in the nation. According to the preservation and history professional on the board of the Frankfort Cemetery, "an unmarked grave was found and [the body was] exhumed, in a cast iron coffin, and smelled heavily of preservatives. It was reburied" (66).

## Rail Development and Unwitting Railroaders

One of the most important products of the Industrial Revolution—the railroads—would facilitate the nation's westward expansion. Construction of twelve miles of rail line between Baltimore and Ellicott's Mills, Maryland, was completed on May 24, 1830, when the line opened for travel. Initially the train consisted of six cars pulled by a single horse; later that year, a steam-powered locomotive replaced the horse (67). Within a short time, this modest beginning would drive great social, economic, and political change within the country. The railroads pushed the frontier westward, expanded the available markets for goods, led to the creation of new towns near their routes, and provided jobs.

Angling would prove to be a major beneficiary of railway development. Before the start of the Civil War, the railways had spread throughout the eastern United States, with the exception of the northern parts of Wisconsin and Michigan, northern Maine, and the majority of Florida. The rails connected major cities from the East Coast to the Mississippi River; in the newly developing Corn Belt, most farms were within five miles of a line. The nineteenth-century railroad offered a swifter, more comfortable transportation to more varied inland destinations than any other method of transport. For the angler, the railroads were now the best way to gain timely access to some of the most desirable fishing waters. The railways also became a means to propagate the fish population to new environments and a way to distribute and transport tackle to previously remote areas.

The railway companies noticed the intensified interest in angling as a sport and began to use innovative, proactive approaches to becoming the anglers' partner in piscatorial excursions. The first step in the process was to develop more angling destinations by stocking game fish in railway-accessible waters (61). A hardy adaptable fish with a fighting attitude was needed—a worthy opponent. When it became known that both largemouth and smallmouth bass were easily adaptable to differences in water types and temperature variations (10), as well as sufficiently hardy to survive rail transportation, railway companies had their champion. Redistribution of the black bass was about to begin.

Originally, the smallmouth bass had a lesser habitat range than that of the largemouth; it was indigenous to the St. Lawrence, Ohio, Tennessee, and upper Mississippi Rivers and the Great Lakes. The largemouth was indigenous to southeastern Canada and much of the eastern United States outside of New England. In any case, the range of the black bass expanded greatly around 1850 when they became unwitting railroaders. General W. W. Shriver first introduced the bass via railroad transport to the mid-Atlantic states in 1854. Fewer than thirty black bass made the initial trip on the Baltimore and Ohio Railroad from the Ohio drainage of West Virginia to the Chesapeake & Ohio Canal, which has free access to the Potomac River and its tributaries (3).

Shriver described relocating bass in large perforated tin buckets designed to fit into the opening of the water tank on the tender car attached to the train's steam locomotive—an ideal method to keep young bass "alive, fresh, and sound" during relocation. After the first transfer, several more occurred that same year, with many unrecorded movements in years following (3). As soon as new rail tracks were laid, the bass were not far behind, usually being stocked by railroad employees or "public-spirited" passengers who traveled with buckets (61). During the 1850s and 1860s, bass were introduced into the New England states, and by 1870, west of the Rockies.

The locomotive's onboard water supply for the steam boiler required replenishment about every 100 to 150 miles. Accordingly, water stations comprising a natural or fabricated basin and water source to fill it were created, usually by damming streams with the railroad grade itself. Water drawn from the ponds was pumped into tall towers alongside the tracks, with the excess simply routed via a spillway under the rails. Once a pond was established, a wetland habitat would form, supporting local wildlife. Bass, pan fish, and pike would soon have a new home there, and should the pond overflow, fish would spill into the downstream creeks and propagate in other waters (61).

The onboard water supply was located in the tender car, immediately behind the number 24 on this locomotive.

## A Successful Transplantation of Black Bass

Following a fishing trip to the Saratoga Springs area of New York in 1859, Professor H. R. Agnel developed a plan to relocate bass from Saratoga Lake to some of the quiet little lakes west of the Hudson River in Orange County, New York. Following through on his idea, the professor struck a deal with an experienced angler to supply sixty live bass, each weighing over a pound and a half, that would be delivered via rail to the West Point depot during the ensuing autumn. The fish made the railway trip successfully, then journeyed three hours by wagon over the rough mountain roads to Woods Lake, their new home. The following August, Professor Agnel returned there to check the status of the fish. But after spending more than a week looking, he was unable to locate any. Agnel described what happened next.

> After more than a week or so, a sense of disappointment was fast stealing over my mind, when one day a neighboring farmer paid me a visit with his two urchins, begging

they might be indulged with a couple of small baithooks for the purpose of taking a few Sunfish with worms. They were speedily accommodated, but had not been gone long before they returned shouting "Daddy, we've cotched two of the queerest fish you ever see!—they ain't Sunfish, they ain't Catfish, and they ain't Yaller Perch, and we dunno what they be!

Agnel identified the fish as two young bass, each 3½ inches long and an inch wide. These fish were part of the first spawning that occurred in February or March. In September 1864 Agnel landed a bass there measuring 18½ inches in length and weighing four pounds, which he identified as being one of the original stocks. He also related that the stocked bass now took the spoon lure readily, rose freely at a fly, and were often caught by still-fishing with minnow or grasshopper (68).

## Vertically Integrated Tackle Manufacturing

America's Industrial Revolution started with Slater's textile mill in Rhode Island. Eighty-two years later, near the end of the revolution, a factory built by Thomas H. Chubb for mass-producing fishing tackle became a fixture in the small town of Post Mills, Vermont. The company, established in 1869, suffered from a fire, and Chubb rebuilt the burned-down factory in the fall of 1875 on the banks of the Ompompanoosuc River (69). Primarily, Chubb manufactured fishing rods and reels.

Alfred W. Miller, writing as Sparse Grey Hackle, provided a commentary on Chubb's factory and made an astute observation regarding its capability: "Although this was a relatively small industrial unit, it is unusual in having such adjuncts as a foundry and machine shop to the main woodworking operation" (11). Miller, obviously aware that tackle manufacturers generally did not maintain heavy machining capabilities or perform smelting, casting, or forging operations to supply their production requirements, knew these types of parts were typically supplier-sourced. Accordingly, he identified the foundry and machine shop, which he called "adjuncts," as "unusual," which they were. A more accurate description would be that the foundry and machine shop were integral components of the original factory design, not additions; they supported a new business strategy whose time had just arrived.

Thos. H. Chubb's factory (from 1891 retail catalogue)

Chubb designed and organized his new factory to support a contemporary nineteenth-century business approach called vertical integration. Most references to the strategy attribute its origin to Andrew Carnegie's Pittsburgh steel mills or Gustavus Swift's Chicago meat-packing empire, because both of these industry titans successfully employed and advocated vertical integration during the latter part of the century. Carnegie, who owned steel companies, purchased iron mines and reserves of coke, a derivative of coal, to supply the raw materials for his smelters. He also bought railroads and ships to transport the material to the mills and deliver the finished product to customers. In this way he controlled the activity, both upstream and downstream, of the steel mill and lowered the cost of steel production.

Chubb employed the same strategy, on a much smaller scale, in 1875—possibly an earlier date than either Carnegie or Swift. Upstream vertical integration offered better control of incoming material to supply production quantity, quality, and delivery requirements than supplier sourcing. To satisfy his need for copious amounts of numerous kinds of brass castings for rods and reels, he built a small on-site foundry so he could produce them rather than buy them. Foundry workers, using scrap metal from the back end of the production process, resmelted and recast brass into new production parts. The advantages for Chubb were direct control of incoming material, higher quality, fewer delays, and reduced cost; his success with this well-planned facility is a quintessential example of vertical integration.

Chubb organized manufacturing processes functionally for his two major product lines, Calcutta bamboo fishing rods and multiplying reels. Rods began processing in the split-bamboo room, where the most specialized equipment in the factory performed complex machining operations to produce the rod blanks. Upon completion, the blanks went to the varnish and shellac room for application of a durable finish, and then to the drying room before moving into the finishing room for installation of rod ferrules and handles. The build process finished in the winding room with installation of silk lapping and line guides.

Multiplying reels, such as Chubb's flagship model, the "Henshall Van Antwerp" black bass reel, began life in the reel room, where exacting metal machining operations produced the major assemblies. These parts moved to the finishing room for incorporation with other parts produced in the brazing room and for final assembly. Finished products moved into either the storeroom or the tackle room to await shipping assignments for delivery throughout the United States and Canada (69). At this point, Chubb used downstream vertical integration to ensure a clear product path to the market by controlling his product distribution channels to the customer.

Chubb's successful implementation of vertical integration leads one to recognize that he was a good strategist and tactician. Supporting this assumption is the fact that he realized vertical integration could not be a viable option for all incoming production requirements: some materials, such as the Calcutta bamboo used for making rods, required supplier sourcing. He may have highly valued the idea of vertically integrating the bamboo material to correct his 50 percent rejection rate on supplier-sourced bamboo (70), but in practice, the new strategy was not feasible. Calcutta bamboo is a tropical and subtropical species native to Southeast Asia, typically not growing anywhere near Post Mills, Vermont. Further, the difficulty of setting up a tropical grow-your-own operation, like a Dole pineapple farm, would not have been viable for his smallish factory. One downside to vertical integration is that if implemented improperly, it is costly to fix; Chubb did avoid that mistake.

The shift to mass production is significant for angling historians because it resulted in increased product availability and reduced costs, which together drove the sport's rapid growth by putting tackle in the hands of the everyday person. Consequently, some historians separate nineteenth-century American tackle manufacturing into two ages: the Smith Age (prior to 1875), when gunsmiths also produced fishing rods, and the Golden Age (1875–1900), when mass production fed the sport.

# The Fading Artisan

When reflecting on how Milam made reels, it becomes apparent that handmade does not mean made without machines; powered tools, such as lathes, were essential for his work. Prior to the advent of electricity and without access to waterpower, Milam used a treadle to turn the spindle of his lathe. Commonly called a foot pedal in twenty-first-century vernacular, the treadle transforms leg power into reciprocating or rotary motion in a machine, such as a weaving loom (reciprocating) or a lathe (rotary). In contrast, the lathes employed in Chubb's industrial factory, although similar in construction to Milam's single tool, were run by a 75 horsepower waterwheel connected to a series of pulleys and belts that powered the machines throughout the facility.

Milam used other human-powered tools. During an interview, Clarence Gayle (another Kentucky reel maker and the subject of Chapter 10) said that Milam used a forming punch and a sledgehammer to produce the end caps of the No. 3 size reel from a single piece of metal (38). A similar part produced with a powered drop hammer in a factory may well be indiscernible from one handmade with a sledgehammer. In the same interview, Gayle also stated that Milam's old friend, B. F. Meek, had the equivalent caps for his Louisville-made reels "punched out at one of the metal plants in the East" (38). By subcontracting with a factory to produce the more simple parts of his handmade reel, Meek had started to blur the meaning of handmade.

By the 1880s, production of fishing reels had already began shifting from artisans single-handedly producing complete products to factory workers repeatedly performing specific functions. When mass production began to be used, the actual manufacturing operations (cutting, grinding, fitting, forming, lapping, etc.) for an equivalent product did not differ substantially between the artisan and factory, other than the fact that the individual artisan typically put more hand finishing and adjusting into the product. However, within a very short period—less than twenty years—the gap between artisan and factory had become significant. Machines capable of holding tighter tolerances and improved manufacturing processes made it possible to produce significant numbers of quality products to exacting specifications.

In a 1905 article written for the sporting goods industry, Clarence Gayle specifically discussed handmade reels and made a good case for their superiority over those made by machines. He acknowledged that eliminating the extra time consumed by manual work methods would cover the cost of putting in machinery to mechanize the process. In spite of this, he maintained that these savings are lost because of the poor product quality resulting from expedited production methods and the use of softer materials, such as brass rather than German silver, to fabricate the parts. He said he would consider adopting machine processes for his own Frankfort shop if his stringent product quality requirements could be maintained, but gave the impression that they could not. He was convinced that limited production numbers incentivized the artisan to take greater care and precision to produce a better product in order to get more pay (71).

Unfortunately for Gayle, the times of the individual artisan were fading away, and he was unable to make a financial success of the reel-making business. By the end of 1905, the same year his article appeared, Gayle shut his shop doors and took a job with the manufacturing tooling department of Buick Motors in Flint, Michigan.

As for the machine-made reel, Chubb's Black Bass Reel was not a cheap reel of dubious quality (the design itself is another topic, but irrelevant to this discussion). It was a high-quality product. When angling customers examined the reel, I strongly suspect they regarded its fit, finish, and overall quality as top-notch; they may not have been able to differentiate it from a handmade one. The transition to mass production was obviously successful, and much credit must pass to Chubb.

Interestingly, vertically integrated companies have continued to be successful throughout the twentieth century and into the twenty-first. The "full stack" approach, in which a single company invents a product, manufactures it and sells it to customers, is popular in Silicon Valley. Apple Computer is a prime example.

The story of how Thos. H. Chubb organized and ran his factory is not an all-inclusive discussion regarding 19th century mass-production of tackle; it is one example. Numerous other manufacturers also made angling gear concurrently with Chubb, using various strategies and processes that fit their particular business models. Some succeeded, others failed. Mergers and acquisitions occurred and that industry boomed.

In 1891, Chubb sold his business to a company originally founded in Pelham, Massachusetts, prior to the Civil War. In later years, known as the Montague Rod and Reel Company, it was probably the oldest mass-producing fishing rod manufacturer in America and it soon became the largest global producer of rods and reels. That statistic, however, obscures the fact that their products were generally invisible to the public because they were trademarked with the names of tackle distributors and retail outlets, not Montague's mark. Nevertheless, unlike the expensive handmade rods and reels produced by artisans, Montague's mass-produced, value-priced rods and reels often cost an angler only a day's wage or less.

As an example, the 1902 Sears, Roebuck & Company catalog offered a line of Pennell fishing reels, a trade name used by Edw. K. Tryon Co. whose reels were frequently produced by Montague. The lowest priced Pennell advertised by Sears, a single action brass reel and therefore unfit for baitcasting, sold for fifteen cents plus six cents postage. A quadruple multiplying Pennell, in principle capable for baitcasting use, sold for $1.75 plus sixty cents postage. Other large American companies like Enterprise Manufacturing (Pflueger), Andrew B. Hendryx, A. F. Meisselbach and Horton often had multiple product lines of varying quality tackle. The inexpensive gear, marketed to target immeasurable numbers of novice baitcasters, drove the exponential growth of the sport.

In 1893, with America's one hundred-year-long Industrial Revolution now nearing its end, Chicago hosted the World's Columbian Exposition, which highlighted achievements of the United States and other nations in a variety of fields, including manufacturing and technology. That event included a Fisheries Pavilion, which prominently featured angling tackle exhibits. Among those was the famed handmade Kentucky reel collection assembled by Henshall. First prize in the fishing reel category, which included both hand- and mass-produced reels, went to B. C. Milam and Son for their now famous handmade Frankfort Kentucky Reel, a hand-powered machine prized by affluent anglers globally.

Yet, the ordinary American Joe would have to settle for the ubiquitous tackle off the assembly line, some of it good quality, some not so; most within a working person's reach.

## Chapter 5

# MID-NINETEENTH-CENTURY BAITCASTING TACKLE

### *1845 to 1880*

## John J. Brown & Company

Prior to 1845, American tackle manufacturers had little to offer the baitcasting angler. John J. Brown published *The American Angler's Guide* that year, and even though he took much of what he wrote from English sources, American anglers welcomed the book. It was a small, unpretentious, pocket-sized manual full of useful information regarding fishing tackle and the practice of angling—information Brown had accumulated by means of his business, John J. Brown & Co.'s Angler's Depot and General Emporium. The store, located at 122 Fulton Street in New York City, sold fishing tackle, fine cutlery, fancy goods, sporting items, and a silver-plating fluid, which he manufactured, for restoring silver finishes (72). Accordingly, with this kind of business experience, it is not surprising that Brown surpassed other American authors of the period with the descriptive value of his work regarding tackle. Regarding the actual practice of angling, however, Brown needed assistance.

In the preface to his book, Brown disclosed that he had decided to publish because American angling literature was hard to come by. His tackle-store business provided him general information, but he needed something more specific on the art of angling. As a result, he consulted with knowledgeable anglers from whom he received "much valuable information" (73). Brown validated that before 1845, helpful practical information was generally nonexistent.

Brown's *Angler's Guide* also provided descriptions and the distribution of the common species of American fish (done naïvely, sometimes erroneously, but par for the period). He also included observations on angling techniques, a discussion on bait, and interesting expositions on tackle of the period—no doubt tackle currently available for sale in his store.

Brown advised that a successful angler would have a complete assortment of tackle. He identified the necessary items in a list of recommended tackle that appears on the following two pages.

# Brown's Recommended Tackle (1845)

The left column lists the tackle that John J. Brown recommended in his 1845 *American Angler's Guide*, quoted verbatim. The right column contains related information compiled from other parts of his guide.

| Recommended Tackle | Related Information |
|---|---|
| Salmon and Trout Rods for both bait and fly-fishing; rods for bass and pickerel; and for bridge fishing and trolling; spare tops of different sizes. | In 1845, black bass and pike rods were noted to be twelve to fifteen feet in length. The single ferruled rod for the novice cost two to five dollars; the one for the scientific angler varied from five to fifty dollars and was made from ash, bamboo, Calcutta reed, or lancewood. There were three requisites for all good rods: strength, lightness, and pliability; it was necessary that the wood have a uniform flexibility from butt to top. |
| Lines of silk, silk and hair twisted and platted, silk-worm gut, India grass; and hemp or flax lines for trolling or fishing. | For salmon, lake pickerel, and black bass, the line was made of flax, hemp, grass, silk, or hair, in lengths of 50 to 200 yards. Line for trout could be made of silk, silk and hair, or fine flax, but was most commonly India grass, in lengths of twelve to twenty yards. |
| Reels or Winches, small and large, for light or heavy fishing. | The best anglers preferred a multiplying reel because it could wind up much faster, allowing them to enjoy more sport in the same length of time. Some objected to the multiplier, believing the wheels of the multiplier were apt to be clogged by friction or bent by pressure. This may have applied to the imported reels, but not to those of American manufacture, whose quality superseded the foreign reels. |
| Hooks of various patterns, from No. 0 to 12, on silk-worm gut, hair, gimp or wire or hemp, &c., snap-hooks for trolling, loose Hooks available in all sizes. | The most common hook in use in this country was the Kirby. "Buy the original. There are many cheap hooks of the Kirby description, imported and sold in this country and many goods imported, and labeled 'manufactured expressly for the American market,' which are absolutely unfit." |

| Recommended Tackle | Related Information |
| --- | --- |
| Floats of quill, cork or wood available in various sizes. | The wood was usually red cedar. Floats were adapted to the current of the water or the peculiar description of angling. They were of two shapes: egg and oblong. |
| Sinkers (plain, swivel and hollow, for sea, middle or bottom fishing), split shot and swivels for fly fishing. | The slide sinker was a thick lead tube, slightly rounded at each end; it allowed line to pass through at the least motion of the fish, which the angler immediately felt. It was considered much better than those sinkers that the fish moved before the angler had notice of his luck. The swivel sinker was best for any fishing; it swiveled at each end, which gave the advantages of "spinning" the bait in trolling and preventing line from twisting. |
| Leaders of hair, gut or grass of various lengths; loose gut for making or repairing leaders or tying on hooks; and gimp or wire for pickerel tackle. | Silkworm gut was taken when the silkworm was about to spin. Little was known about this extraordinary substance except among dealers and scientific anglers. The best silkworm gut was made in Spain; inferior qualities were made in China and Italy. |
| Squids of pearl for trolling, artificial flies, minnows, grasshoppers, frogs, mice, shrimp. | Great improvements had been made within the previous few years in the manufacture of artificial baits. |
| Disgorgers of various sizes, bait needles, clearing rings, bait and landing nets, bait box, and baskets. | |
| A Book with an assortment of artificial flies, a box with a variety of feathers, worsted, silks, gold thread, wax. | |
| A pair of pliers, a pair of scissors, a penknife, hand vice, and a file for sharpening the points and barbs of hooks. | |

# J. T. Buel and the Spoon

In his 1865 book *Superior Fishing*, Robert Barnwell Roosevelt maintained that "the black bass prefers the fly, but will take the trolling-spoon" (74). The "spoon," invented by Julio Thompson (J. T.) Buel and in continuous use by anglers since 1848, has a reputation with many anglers as one of the most effective artificial lures ever produced. The earliest editions of Brown's book did not mention the spoon because at the time it was still unknown. Interestingly, Brown's fourth edition of *The Angler's Guide*, published in 1857, had a single illustration of a spoon; it appears to be an early knockoff of the Buel product.

Julio Thompson Buel was born in 1806 and raised in Castleton, Vermont. His father was a furrier who taught him the trade and how to fish. The elder Buel kept a small boat that Julio used for fishing in the western part of Vermont on Lake Bomoseen, which was known for large trout.

In the boat one day, drifting and eating his lunch, the young Buel accidently dropped his spoon into the lake. As he watched it spiral downward, he saw a large fish grab it and swim away. Julio had an inspiration, and angling would never be the same. Returning home, he took another of his mother's spoons, sawed off the handle, soldered a hook to the concave side, and drilled a hole in the opposite end.

The next morning he tied his new lure to a line and proceeded to troll it around the lake until he landed two extremely large trout. Later that day the young man showed his catch to the town folks of Castleton. They were amazed. Buel's neighbors had never used anything but natural bait, but that would soon change as Buel began making spoons for local anglers.

A few years before Buel's revelation, Henry Herbert emigrated from England to New York and began writing outdoor articles under the pen name of Frank Forester. Buel became an avid reader of Herbert's writing. As a result, Buel sent a number of his spoons to Herbert, who used them with great success. Later Herbert praised the success of Buel's spoons in *Spirit of the Times*, an early sportsman's publication, and the popularity of the lure soared.

In 1848 Buel began making angling spoons full-time in Whitehall, New York. Because of Herbert's enthusiastic promotion, the demand for the new lures was enormous, and Buel was persistently behind in filling the orders. Even so, he refused to reduce backlog by compromising the quality of his product; he continued using the finest materials and highest standards of production quality possible. Due to the effectiveness and durability of Buel's spoons, the backlog grew as orders continued to pour in.

Early J. T. Buel spoon with 1854 patent date

(Courtesy of Skenesborough Museum, Whitehall, New York)

In his book *19th Century Fishing Lures*, Arlan Carter devoted a complete and highly descriptive chapter to the lures made by J. T. Buel. Carter noted that Buel received the first patent ever granted for a fishing lure, US Patent 8,852, on April 6, 1852. Four more patents followed, including an 1854 patent for a weedless hook and an 1876 patent for a spreading device to allow the use of two spoons on one line (75). At the nation's Centennial Celebration in Philadelphia in 1876, Buel received a medal in recognition of his contribution to the sport of American fishing. He sold his business in 1885 due to poor health and died in May 1886.

On October 13, 1967, the Eppinger Manufacturing Company of Dearborn, Michigan, maker of the Dardevle spoon, acquired the rights to produce Buel's products (76). It was a perfect fit. Family-owned since 1906 and one of the oldest tackle manufacturers in America, Eppinger Manufacturing is known for the meticulous quality and effectiveness of its tackle. It produces Buel lures in three different sizes, both weighted and unweighted, in an astounding variety of finishes.

The photo on the next page showing the 21st century Eppinger spoon is noteworthy. The spoon, stamped with Buel tool dies, interestingly employs a friendly competitor's (G. M. Skinner) innovation: flutes for causing refractory light rays. Originally part of Skinner's 1874 patent, this feature became available to copy when the patent expired.

Eppinger Manufacturing Company's modern Buel spoon

## Trolling the Spoon

Buel's spoon was a hot product in the mid-nineteenth century and a topic of debate among those who believed it too effective. Early anglers employed the spoon successfully while trolling; as a result, the spoon, the technique, and the anglers all received criticism. Even as recently as the twenty-first century, some anglers consider freshwater trolling as less sporting than other techniques. The practice has not changed significantly since the invention of the outboard motor (about 1900). Many anglers have trolled a lure from time to time, alone in the boat or not, with a gas-powered outboard or (since the mid-1930s) an electric trolling motor slowly putt-putting over productive fish structure with a lure trailing in the water to attract a strike.

Thaddeus Norris, writing in the mid-nineteenth century, described trolling very differently. Norris alleged that trolling with a spoon does not afford the pleasure that still-fishing from the shore does because no skill is required to find the fish; that is done by the boatman who is familiar with the lake. He believed that a mere novice would catch as many fish when trolling as an expert angler, and therefore trolling with a spoon was "unsportsmanlike" (68).

Robert B. Roosevelt, in his 1862 book *Game Fish of Northern States*, took a different view and recommended Buel's spoon. "A small trolling spoon is excellent bait, probably preferable to the fly at all seasons except the middle of July, when the eel-fly, the principal food of the bass, is just disappearing.... In case a spoon is used, the shank of the hook is usually wound with ibis feathers, and a Buel's patent is the favorite" (77).

Buel spoons

## Early Lures Were Limited in Type and Effectiveness

The selection of artificial baitcasting lures other than spoons, spinners, and similar metal baits was slim during the years immediately following the Civil War. However, a number were available and used by anglers in the 1860s. We can discern from the words of Roosevelt in his book *Superior Fishing* that some of the new artificial lures of the period lacked the effectiveness of Buel's spoon. "Efforts have been continually made to make artificial representations of the other food and baits for fish; exact and beautiful copies of grasshoppers and frogs have been constructed, and painted of the proper color, but either from the nature of the composition or some other cause, entirely in vain.... It is doubtful whether any fish was ever captured with such delusions.... Although they are still retained in the shops, they no longer find a place amid the angler's paraphernalia" (74).

Roosevelt discussed lures that imitate fish and advised that "the imitation fish itself has, until late years, invariably proved a failure." However, he maintained that with the discovery of gutta-percha, an early plastic first used in 1845 and made from the latex of several Malaysian trees, lures improved. "A little fish made of this material is not only a faultless imitation of the original, and is even curved in a way to produce the most perfect spin, but being soft to the teeth, seems absolutely to convince the trout in spite of their palates that it is wholesome and appropriate food." Roosevelt also described a modification to the lure that entailed adding "two tin flanges at the head... and leaving the body straight.... This invention is extremely light, being hollow.... In its present perfected form, it is a foreign production, but the original discovery was American" (74). The first minnow he described may have been a gutta-percha Trout

Bait No. 83, sold by the S. Allcock Company of Redditch, England; the second, possibly a Phantom Minnow, also sold by Allcock. Both English lures fit Roosevelt's description and would have been available at the time.

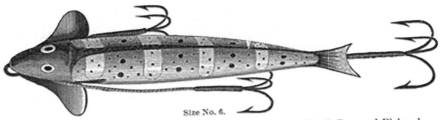

## Celebrated Phantom Minnow.

Size No. 6.

Made of Silk, coated with Rubber, very light, very fine for Black Bass and Pickerel.

## Riley Haskell's Minnow

In the fraternity of twenty-first-century fishing lure collectors, the most famous early lure from this period (1848–1875) is probably the Haskell Minnow, produced by Riley Haskell and patented on September 20, 1859. Haskell, a gunsmith living in Painesville, Ohio, was a master artisan capable of not only repairing rifles but also manufacturing them. When Haskell decided to produce his "Trolling Bait," he went first-class all the way. The minnow-shaped lures are made of copper and brass soldered together. The quality and attention to detail are exquisite. The lure has fins, a tail, and a scale pattern on the body; the lower portion of the body rotates as it travels through the water. Collectors originally believed that Haskell made these works of art in three sizes: 3 inches, 4½ inches, and 5½ inches long; but later a 10-inch version that had been hidden away for decades surfaced, revealing that he also made a muskie-size lure. The only known example of the ten-inch version of this lure sold at auction on November 18, 2003, for $101,200, the highest price ever paid for a fishing tackle collectable.

In his 1875 book *Fishing in American Waters*, Genio C. Scott briefly commented on Haskell's minnow. Scott said the lure could be purchased in most fishing tackle stores. Regarding the lure's effectiveness, he reported that the feedback he received concerning the bait was positive and he believed it would serve well if used on the lakes in the Adirondacks and the waters surrounding the Thousand Islands (78).

The Haskell Minnow

(Courtesy of the History of Fishing Museum, Branson, MO)

## Rods and Reels

Around 1860, gunsmiths like Riley Haskell often produced various angling products, especially fishing rods. Other rod makers, like Thaddeus Norris, were avid anglers as well as masters in the crafts. In his 1939 history *Angling in America*, Goodspeed pointed out that both the rods made by Norris and his personal rod-building techniques, described within the chapters of his book about the time split bamboo first came into use, were highly valued by early anglers (5). Charles M. Wetzel, in his bibliography *American Fishing Books*, noted that Norris, unsurpassed in this art, may have invented the first split bamboo rod in America, or if not, was certainly capable of doing so (79). Samuel Philippe, a gunsmith of Easton, Pennsylvania, is generally recognized as having constructed the first bamboo rod using six-strip sections, but this too is not certain. Regardless, the fact that Norris was a highly competent producer of rods makes his advice about rods especially valuable.

On behalf of anglers who could afford only one fishing rod, Norris recommended a "general" rod with a hollow butt to store various sizes and weights of rod tips for bait fishing and trolling. Typically produced in five two-foot hickory wood sections, a serviceable one sold for three to four dollars. Dame, Stoddard & Kendall, a Boston importer and manufacturer, marketed a fine nine-foot general bass rod, a quality rod that cost seven dollars in Lancewood and eight dollars if made in Greenheart. Norris maintained that as a rule, American rods were equal to English rods but in many respects better adapted to the requirements of American anglers. Specifically, Norris identified the American metal rod tip and line guides as being much preferred over the English method of using rings for the line to pass through and a wire loop at the tip. Norris believed this improvement was indispensable, especially on the bass, pike, and trolling rods, because the line passed through with less friction and was less apt to tangle when casting.

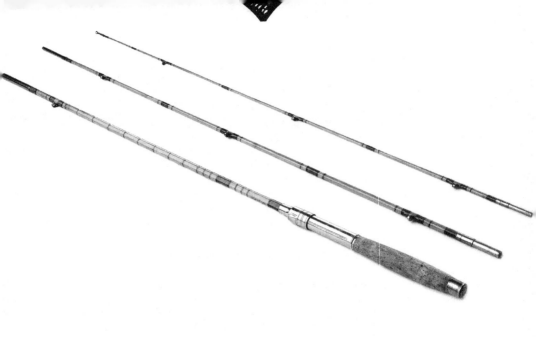

Bait Rod (8-feet 10-inches in long)

The Kentucky multiplying reels were highly popular if one could afford them, but many anglers could not. Norris said that the balance handle, an American invention that used a counterweight or balance weight on the end of the reel crank opposite from the handle, was important to keep the momentum of the bait up during the cast, a popular belief of that period. He noted that the bearings of the costly reels were made of jewels; however, he knew of a reel made by an amateur mechanic (likely J. L. Sage) without jewels that would spin for a minute and a half. According to Norris, the best anglers considered the multiplying reel indispensable for bass in order to make long casts because the line ran out as freely as possible. Norris also noted that in all cases, a short axle is preferable over the long axles used on the old form of the reel because it facilitates winding the line on the spool more quickly and more compactly. Finally, he claimed that "a well-made reel does not jar or clatter, but while the journals fit nicely, they run easily in their bearings, and the inner plates of the spool revolve without friction in the outer" (68).

B. C. Milam No. 4 reel from mid-1880s

For the most part, the store-bought tackle available to the mid-nine-teenth-century angler was understandably sparse, because American tackle entrepreneurs like Thomas Chubb (discussed in Chapter 4) were just starting to implement mass production. To extend the sport's popularity, availability of fishing tackle in copious amounts was necessary, and the process to obtain it had definitely begun.

Beyond tackle, baitcasting needed a defined angling method and a strong cadre of avid, influential, and vocal adherents capable of spreading the new gospel of American sport fishing. The circumstances of the Civil War brought them together in Kentucky.

Ms J. G. McCarthy with 38-pound
Musky she landed, 1916.

(From the book Lake and Stream Game
Fishing by Dixie Carroll)

# Chapter 6

# TRANSITION TO BAITCASTING AS A SPORT

*1815 to 1881*

## Minnow Casting

When the Civil War in the United States began on April 12, 1861, many of the country's physicians were required to relocate to the war front. As a result, Dr. Henshall responded to an urgent call for a surgeon in Cynthiana, Kentucky, in the Bluegrass area about thirty miles north of Lexington. There he provided medical services for the town and surrounding area and, he later wrote, "met and fished with many brothers of the angle who had made the art of black bass fishing famous. They used the 'Frankfort' reel and a short, supple cane rod. A few were fly-fishers, but most of them were bait fishers." At every available opportunity, Henshall fished the local waters. A druggist in town—David M. Snyder, son of George Snyder—loaned Henshall his father's favorite reel until he could have one made in Frankfort. With the borrowed reel, Henshall experienced some of the best black bass fishing in the country (39).

During his time in Kentucky, Henshall practiced a technique known as minnow casting—that is, baitcasting using live bait—when angling for black bass. In the first edition of his *Book of the Black Bass*, published in 1881, he described the application of the technique.

> After casting the minnow, and it alights in a favorable spot, it should be left for a longer or shorter time, depending on the nature of the water fished, and upon the abundance, scarcity, and mood of the Bass. As the line slackens, it should be reeled in slowly until the entire line is retrieved. Sometimes, when fish are plentiful and biting eagerly, it is best to make frequent casts, reeling in rapidly after each cast... so as to give a rapid swimming motion to the bait.... From the time a Bass first "bites" until he is in the landing-net, he should never be given an inch of slack line, under any circumstances. (29)

# Snyder's Reel Invented for Still-Fishing

In 1889 Henshall revealed an obscure fact related to the Kentucky multiplying reel that made minnow casting possible.

> The manufacture of the now famous Kentucky reel was first begun forty some years ago.... The reel was originally made for bait-fishing only.... It was invented to meet the requirements of still fishing, where the butt of the cane rod was frequently stuck in the bank (often by a spike provided for that purpose), thus relieving the lazy angler of holding the rod or watching his float while waiting for "a bite," until the singing of the "alarm" announced that welcome contingency. (32)

I was taken aback by the words "originally made for bait-fishing only" and "invented to meet the requirements of still fishing." The information was hard for me to believe, because Snyder's little hand-powered machine for casting, retrieving, and storing line was the perfect and necessary tool for the sport of baitcasting.

If George Snyder specifically made the first multiplying reel for still-fishing, when did the baitcasting method come into use?

Some historians might say the method came into use immediately, because the problematic part of making the change from still-fishing to baitcasting was in developing the reel. Once the reel became available, all that remained was to change the technique for retrieving the bait. It could be as easy as this: while still-fishing a minnow, no bites occur. The angler, wondering if bait remains on the hook, starts the retrieve to check the bait. A fish strikes, a "Hallelujah!" moment occurs, and a new technique is born. Surely it would be hard to believe that the seasoned Kentucky river anglers of Snyder's day had not discovered the solution for minnow casting; first, because the method was a natural extension of the inherent capability of the reel, and second, because it seems unlikely that veteran anglers lacked sufficient imagination to retrieve a lip-hooked minnow for imitating moving prey. However, finding evidence that documents the change turned out to be difficult.

## In 1857, Silverside's Method Was Still-Fishing

Very little angling literature, scholarly or popular, was published prior to the Civil War. Thus the documentation describing early nineteenth-century Kentucky bait angling techniques is almost invisible. I did, however, find a single relevant three-thousand-word article in one of the few periodicals from that era that published angling articles:

*Porter's Spirit of the Times*, a weekly New York City paper with a circulation of about twenty-two thousand copies. The article, entitled "Bass and Bass Fishing," was written by a Kentucky author using the pen name "Silverside" and published on March 21, 1857. This scarce piece of writing is a fine example of useful early bait-fishing popular literature.

Silverside came close to describing the new method of baitcasting, but fell short: the technique of retrieving the bait via the reel to imitate prey was missing. Silverside's method was to cast a minnow upstream and allow the current to move the bait into fertile water below, but no retrieve follows. Once the bait floated to the end of its tether, it remained there awaiting a bite. Besides, Silverside declared that if the water is very clear and still, one should fasten the rod into the bank, adjust the alarm wheel of the spool, and retire from the shore—the old Kentucky still-fishing technique that Henshall derided in the 1889 quote above. The article also noted that an angler might patiently occupy a position for an entire day and receive no reward, not even a solitary nibble, even though the bass may be felt toying with the bait (80). That article, written by a very competent and educated individual, described still-fishing, not baitcasting.

## First Documented Use of the Baitcasting Method

Not yet having a definitive answer for when the baitcasting method came into use, I returned to Henshall's autobiography. There I found valuable information within his description of catching his first bass.

> On the Fourth of July, 1855... I hooked a minnow through the lips.... I waded out far enough to reach the current and threw in the bait, allowing it to float down-stream by stripping a few yards from the reel.... I reeled in the bait slowly for another cast and as it came within view I observed a fine fish following it, but seeing me he backed slowly down the stream.... [I] cast again, as well as I could with a click reel, farther out in the stream.... When the bait floated down the length of the line it swerved with the current to the rock first mentioned, and I began to reel it in very leisurely. Again I saw the bass following it, but seeing me he desisted as before. I cast again toward the flat rock, and when the minnow floated to the end of its tether I began reeling as rapidly as I could when the bass, not to be foiled again, made a vicious lunge and seized the bait. Then followed a battle that I will never forget. (39)

Before ever having seen a multiplying reel, Henshall managed to stumble upon the necessary technique using a single-action click reel.

Consequently, he surely suspected that by retrieving the bait after a cast he was on to something important. In the same chapter of his autobiography Henshall wrote, "A fish [bass] so fully endowed... made it necessary for me to adopt an entirely different plan of fishing from that to which I had become accustomed" (39).

During the summer and autumn of 1856, Henshall fished on the same stream. One day he noticed an elderly man "owing to the long distance to which he cast his minnow, and the rapidity with which he reeled it in again." Henshall questioned him "as to his long casting and rapid retrieving, which he said was due to his excellent reel. The reel, he explained, was a multiplier of very fine workmanship made by an expert watchmaker and silversmith in Frankfort, Kentucky, and was known as the Frankfort reel; it was used by a few anglers in Kentucky, southern Ohio and Indiana. He added that it cost twenty-five dollars, but he considered it cheap at the price." Five years later, when Henshall relocated to Cynthiana, Kentucky, he used a similar reel when he fished with those who "had made the art of black bass fishing famous" (39).

By the beginning of the Civil War, when baitcasting tools, methods, and technically competent practitioners coalesced in Kentucky, the sport of baitcasting was a reality. Documented confirmation is lacking, but there is no doubt that Kentucky anglers did engage in baitcasting prior to Henshall's appearance there in 1861; believing otherwise would be misguided due to the utter simplicity of the transition. At this writing (2016), the earliest documented date of baitcasting is Henshall's angling activity on Wednesday, July 4, 1855 (recorded in 1920 as an autobiographical recollection). By 1884, when Henshall promoted an event for casting the minnow at the National Rod and Reel Association casting tournament, baitcasting was a national sport (3). In his 1887 book *The Art of Angling*, Wakeman Holberton said the "new and very sporting way of angling for Black Bass" began to proliferate rapidly (81). By 1889 minnow casting was firmly established as an original American method of angling (32).

## Early Propagation of the Sport:
## Four Well-Connected Anglers

For baitcasting to emerge as a national sport, it needed to propagate from the Bluegrass region of Kentucky across the rest of the nation. Initially, a significant obstacle was the scarcity and cost of a Kentucky Reel; the anglers who could meet the expense of one tended to be prominent upper-class individuals. Luckily, history permanently records the activities of such people. The following account involves three famous Kentuckians—Mason Brown, Francis Preston Blair Sr., and Henry Clay—and a US president from New York, Martin Van Buren.

# THE GREAT NATIONAL FISHING MATCH.

## "THE RESULT."

## Mason Brown (1799–1867)

Mason Brown, a devoted angler and fishing partner of J. F. Meek, is the least well known of this group of anglers except in the world of Kentucky baitcasting reels. The Brown family entertained graciously at Liberty Hall, their Frankfort home. Some of the Browns' guests included the Marquis de Lafayette, President James Monroe, and future presidents Andrew Jackson and Zachary Taylor (82). Brown was appointed a judge for the Kentucky circuit bench in 1839 and held that position for ten years. From 1855 to 1859 Brown served as Kentucky's Secretary of State.

## Francis Preston Blair Sr. (1791–1876)

Raised in Frankfort, Francis Preston Blair Sr. was Mason Brown's second cousin and sometime companion (83). He was an angling partner of President Martin Van Buren and was also well known by Henry Clay. One of the most powerful politicians in America, Blair was an advisor and confidante to Abraham Lincoln and founded the Republican Party. (Actor Hal Holbrook played Francis Blair in Steven Spielberg's 2012 motion picture *Lincoln*.)

Mason Brown

(Courtesy of Liberty Hall Historic Site, Frankfort, Kentucky)

Francis Preston Blair, Sr.

(Courtesy of Blair House, the President's Guest House, US Department of State)

### Henry Clay (1777–1852)

Sage suggested that one of the anglers in the Clay family might have initially persuaded Snyder to produce a multiplying reel. In 1815 the best-known member of the Clays was thirty-eight-year-old Henry, a US senator who had previously been Speaker of the House of Representatives. Although it remains unknown whether Henry, an angling mate of Van Buren, ever owned a Snyder-made reel, there is little doubt that he was familiar with the multiplier. On February 1, 1821, Snyder produced one for Brutus Clay, Henry's cousin. Clay also had a long and documented relationship with Mason Brown, the owner of the first Meek reel.

### Martin Van Buren (1782–1862)

Eighth president of the United States of America from 1837 to 1841, Martin Van Buren was an avid angler from Kinderhook, New York, but he has garnered no respect for his angling prowess, an injustice. In a late-twentieth-century book examining presidential anglers, Van Buren's history remained absent but for one comment: "George Washington fished for recreation… but… we wouldn't rank him much higher than John Quincy Adams or Martin Van Buren" (84). (Regarding Adams, his wife was the angler, not the president himself.)

Henry Clay

(Courtesy of the Ashland
Estate Historic Site)

President Martin Van Buren

(Courtesy of the
Library of Congress)

# Anglers of Lindenwald, the Van Buren Home (1842–1849)

Henry Clay was an angling partner of Martin Van Buren. The latter visited Clay's Kentucky home, Ashland, in Lexington the week of May 20, 1842, for recreation; Clay stated that they did not discuss politics (85). Likewise, Clay stayed at Van Buren's home, Lindenwald, in Kinderhook, New York, on multiple occasions during the mid-1840s (85) (86) (87), where the men definitely angled together as partners (88).

A number of interesting stories about angling at Lindenwald exist, and one specifically involves Clay. It seems that President Van Buren, accompanied by Clay and several other Lindenwald fishing guests, asked young John Cooney (son of Van Buren's land and farm operations manager, Patrick J. Cooney) to gather some bait for the next day's angling. The boy let Van Buren know that he did not wish to trap minnows for the outing because the president had failed to pay him for the previous week's bait.

Van Buren quipped, "But you supplied no minnows that day." The boy retorted that he had worked hard to catch minnows, but the creek's high water level had prevented their capture. Van Buren's guests within earshot of the conversation began to roar with laughter and started to make fun at the president's expense. Clay then proceeded to give the boy a dollar, remarking that the lad argued his point well, and suggested that the boy would make a good lawyer. The other anglers followed Clay's example and contributed eight to ten dollars more for the boy's bait payment, guaranteeing the desired minnows for the next day (88).

The Martin Van Buren National Historic Site at Kinderhook, New York, has a delightful display of period-correct baitcasting tackle to represent the equipment Van Buren angled with when he lived at Lindenwald. The rod, reel, and lures displayed there, constructed by twenty-first-century American artisans, are a tribute to the president's piscatorial passion. This cannot go unnoticed when visiting Van Buren's two fishing ponds. It is certainly possible that Van Buren angled with this type of equipment; however, I personally do not believe that he did. The New York reel was not the "exquisitely machined tool that the Kentucky watchmakers produced" (36). It was larger and chunkier than the Kentucky style and had a reel base generally constructed from a single, heavy, machined casting. Most often (unlike the modern New York reel example shown below) the style of the crank handle was counterbalanced with a ball-shaped counterweight on one end and a wooden crank knob on the other. I think the president's technique and equipment modeled the Kentucky style of angling and that he most likely employed a reel made by B. C. Milam, a reel that predated the New York type and was available in 1842–48 when Van Buren and Clay angled together.

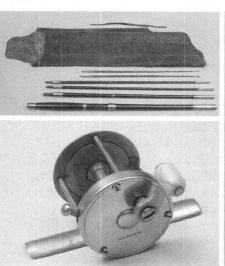
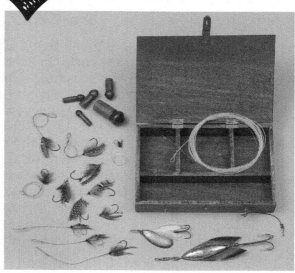

(Courtesy of the Martin Van Buren National Historic Site, Kinderhook, New York)

## Francis Preston Blair Sr. and Martin Van Buren, Angling Partners (1851)

On August 7, 1851, Van Buren wrote a letter to a fellow angler regarding some details about a short fishing trip they had planned. He noted that he had also forwarded the details of their angling plan to "Mr. Blair." He presumed that Blair, in preparation for the trip, would "break the tackle stores in New York," but that he would be satisfied with the tackle provided to him. Van Buren informed his fishing partner that he would be angling for muskellunge on the trip; more interestingly, he revealed that his success in landing just one muskie would provide him sufficient angling success for the whole year (75).

## Baitcasting: A Proliferating Reality

Personally and closely connected, Martin Van Buren, Henry Clay, Francis Blair, and Mason Brown were bait fishers and, by reasonable conjecture, baitcasters. These powerful, influential, and wealthy Americans, all lawyers by profession, operated at the top levels of the government and society; all angled during the transition of still-fishing to baitcasting. Highly mobile, with vast circles of friends, acquaintances, and resources, these men were the power brokers of their time and part of the driving force necessary to promote baitcasting as a new sport.

It is interesting to scan through Henry Clay's schedule on one of his trips to visit Van Buren in New York. On February 23, 1848, he departed for Philadelphia on the five o'clock train. Upon arrival, he rode to the mayor's residence and later delivered a eulogy at Independence Hall for his late friend, former president John Quincy Adams. Clay departed Philadelphia to spend six days in New York City. During that time, he visited Albert Gallatin (senator, ambassador to both France and Great Britain, and US secretary of the treasury), former president Martin Van Buren, and John Jacob Astor (one of the three all-time wealthiest Americans). Here we have a glimpse of the circles Clay traveled in. Adams was not an angler, and it is unknown whether Gallatin or Astor ever angled; other friends and acquaintances of Clay did (86). As Sparse Grey Hackle pointed out, "Angling has always been primarily a sport of sophisticated city dwellers" (70).

The enormous influence and reach that individuals like Van Buren, Clay, Blair, and Brown possessed is difficult for most individuals to fathom. Their prominence alone lent much credence to their words. Like most avid anglers, they no doubt were always eager to communicate their piscatorial successes and opinions. Baitcasting prospered prior to the Civil War in part because influential and famous people angled, discussed tackle and techniques, and told fishing stories while other anglers listened and learned. In addition, the proliferating reality of the transition from still-fishing to the sport of baitcasting was about to be ignited by the campfire discussions of untold numbers of Civil War veterans who returned home to angle.

## The Birth of Baitcasting as a Sport

The age of baitcasting began with the manufacture of Snyder's first reel, which set off a transformation from the angling method of still-fishing to that of baitcasting. Sixty-six years later, on the first day of May, 1881, Henshall began to distribute the first printing of *Book of the Black Bass* to the subscriber list of those who had pre-purchased it (89). The best, truest, and most honorable thing that can be said about the question of when the sport of baitcasting began is this: on Sunday, May 1, 1881, Dr. James Alexander Henshall, Apostle of the Black Bass, announced its birth.

*Yours truly*

*J. A. Henshall,*

(From the Book of the Black Bass)

A Trevor Thomas Fowler painting of Orlando Brown Jr.,
his brother Mason, and their dog Judge, 1844

(Courtesy of Liberty Hall Historic Site, Frankfort, Kentucky)

# Chapter 7
# A CODE OF AMERICAN SPORT ANGLING

*1850 to 1890*

## Protecting the Fish by Developing Moral Anglers

Unrestrained freedom in America to fish at an individual's pleasure, at any time and by whatever means available, put the fish population in danger of annihilation. Somehow, acceptable behaviors for fishing had to defined, quantified, and instilled in the general populace. America initially lacked the infrastructure to accomplish that task, so the responsibility fell on the shoulders of cultivated American angling authors and the press that produced mass periodicals. Many refined American authors were of English descent and familiar with the angling code proffered by the well-bred English anglers. Not surprisingly, the writers saw an opportunity to create an American angling code, and the new American periodicals became their vehicle of expression.

When the pens started hitting paper just prior to 1850, well-educated and well-intentioned upper-class angling authors started their work of defining acceptable sporting behaviors not by drafting proposed legal statutes, but rather by appealing to one's character. Refined Britons angled for game fish by fly-casting, while others angled for coarse fish by bait fishing; therefore, it seemed obvious that the code should delineate the noble qualities that constitute a true sports angler as well as the attributes of the creditable fish to be pursued.

Accordingly, the authors began assessing the various North American fish species in order to judge and rank them as to their game worthiness. Often this meant drawing distinctions and comparisons between species that, in a roundabout way, could reflect descriptively on the social status of various groups of anglers—a slippery slope. Not surprisingly, contentious debates ensued.

Henry William Herbert, an Englishman educated at Eton and Cambridge, came to America in 1831 at the age of thirty-four. He was a prolific novelist and scholar but most famous for his sporting articles, written under the pen name "Frank Forester." An avid sportsman and an expert with both rod and gun, Herbert was a strong voice for instilling sporting values into the hearts of American anglers. He stood between the time when only the upper class practiced the British methods of fishing and a later time when broad segments of the American population angled sportingly.

In the introductory remarks of his book *Fish and Fishing*, Herbert advised his readers that if they fished with a spear, net, setline, or through a hole in the ice, they would be disappointed with his book, because he considered none of these to be sporting. As a sporting individual himself, Herbert recognized only fly-fishing, trolling, and spinning a live minnow (baitcasting with a minnow before the general availability of artificial lures) as being worthy sports. In addition, similar to William Henry Scott, he ranked the number of fish caught as less important than the difficulty of capture (90).

Beyond identifying acceptable fishing methods, Herbert developed an argument for which type of fish constituted game fish. For a fish to be game it must, beyond any basic nutritional value, provide the angler with an exciting fight and be difficult to capture: "Not by taste alone should game fish be known, but by their character" (90). Herbert ranked the salmon above all other fish, including the equivalently sized muskellunge. He identified the latter as having an inferior intellect because it may be caught using flax line, whereas line of fine silk gut was required for the salmon.

Another nineteenth-century author, the much beloved Thaddeus Norris—also known as "the American Walton" or "Uncle Thad"—defined the qualities of the "true angler" somewhat differently than Herbert. Similar to other authors, Norris strongly rejected, in all instances, the use of netting, spearing, snaring, and using setlines to catch fish (68). However, Norris maintained that when fly-casting was not available, the true angler would pursue sunfish or roach and find pleasure in catching them, and he would not spurn the sport of the humbler brother that makes good use of a worm. The ideal angler is "modest" and "quietly self-reliant" (68), a person who considers it a success to take fish when they are difficult to catch. The respectable angler derives enjoyment not only from catching fish but also from enjoying the peaceful inspiration of the art itself.

# Minnesota: Home of Ten Thousand Lakes and Game Thieves

In a short time, it became apparent that no discussion of moral virtues alone would save the fish; regulatory controls over fishing activities at the state level were necessary. Minnesota was a prime example. For an angler in the mid-nineteenth century, the species, range, and quantity of fish available in the Ten Thousand Lakes region became a true vision of heaven, and it was not a secret of the elite. The following excerpt from one of the letters written by Oliver Gibbs to General Spinner, a Civil War general, provides a glimpse of the angling available in Minnesota.

> Dear General... The traveler from the Eastern or Southern States who wishes to imbibe the fullest and grandest... along the route of the Pacific Railroad... where the greatest variety of freshwater game-fish that can be found in any one neighborhood can be taken... I would commend Lake Pepin.... But how about the fishing?... I caught in one day, in Bush River, thirteen trout before breakfast... a twenty-four-pound basket full before dinner, and... thirty... before dark. (91)

The same angling periodicals employed to facilitate the ongoing arguments of what constitutes a game fish or what moral qualities are required of the true angler also publicized the fishing hot spots now speedily accessible via the newly established train system. Prior to 1858, when Minnesota became a state, its ten thousand lakes (actually closer to fifteen thousand) remained completely unregulated and available to all comers, both the sport-minded and the ethically challenged.

In 1858 the new state legislature established laws prohibiting the netting of trout (92). By 1874 the legislature set up a board of fish commissioners with responsibility for the artificial propagation and stocking of fish. The Game and Fish Commission of Minnesota, established by state law in 1891, issued its first annual report to the governor covering the period July 31, 1890, to November 30, 1891. The report indicated that the new commission's board had appointed the first state game warden and authorized four deputy wardens; however, the state lacked the funds to hire the new deputies. As a result, the board appointed special or local wardens in the several counties, when and where needed. (93). They received payment for expenses but no stipend. Nonetheless, increased enforcement efforts kept them busy because, similar to a bounty hunter approach, the local wardens received reward payments for information used in the conviction of game law offenders.

# The Anglers Character and the Fish's Attributes

Interestingly, the Game and Fish Commission's report described the moral characteristics of various types of individuals apprehended as game law violators. In the left column of the following table are verbatim quotations from the annual report to the governor in 1892. The right column lists the attributes of game fish as described in the 1873 book *The Fishing Tourist* by Charles Hallock, longtime editor of *Field & Stream* magazine. Reading the descriptions of Minnesota game law violators and fish species provides insight into the circuitous way mid-nineteenth-century angling authors equated various groups of anglers with game fish.

Fishing party showing off fish caught in Detroit Lake

(Courtesy of the Minnesota State Historical Society)

| Violation Excerpts from the *Report of the Game and Fish Commission of Minnesota* (93) | Game Fish Attributes from *The Fishing Tourist* by Charles Hallock (94) |
|---|---|
| "There is an element... wild and lawless... a class of fellows and not always young fellows.... They are not sportsmen; they are not even game lovers; there is no generous spark within their breasts. The thought that any game should have any chance for life never comes within the little circle of their natures... these game assassins." | "No fish which inhabit foul or sluggish waters can be 'game-fish.' It is impossible from every circumstance of their surroundings and associations. They may flash with tinsel and tawdry attire; they may strike with the brute force of a black-smith, or exhibit the dexterity of a prize-fighter, but their low breeding and vulgar quality cannot be mistaken. Their haunts, their food and manner of eating, betray their grossness." |
| "The next in gravity of offenders are persons who ought to and do know better; they associate with sportsmen and other gentlemen frequently and even pass current as such.... They do not like to be arrested and fined any better than the less cultured... and are beginning to be more careful... as they find they are shown no favors on account of their social position and affected influence." | 'There are some kinds of fish, comely in appearance, bold biters, and rather successful torturers of fine tackle, which are styled game-fish and angled for as such, but which by no means deserve the name and reputation. Such customers may possibly 'pass in a crowd,' as the shabby genteel frequently do among the masses of society." |
| The greatest injury and destruction of the game and fish resources... are perpetrated by professional... fishermen, who are simply organized bandits sent out by fish and game dealers.... They use every forbidden and evil device known to the craft, to secure game in quantities." | "There is no flesh of fish so rank and repulsive to the taste as that of the trout inhabiting a muddy pond where pickerel, bull-heads and slimy eels do congregate.... The trout will become degen-erate, and bear the traits and marks of the evil company he keeps and the unhappy place he calls his home." |

# Robert Barnwell Roosevelt

Of all those who helped make America a better place for angling, one individual in particular deserves special notice for his exemplary contribution: Robert Barnwell Roosevelt. You may also see his middle name spelled as "Barnhill," a name he was born with and later changed to prevent political adversaries from referring to him as "Manure Pile," an unfortunate tag for such a remarkable individual.

Roosevelt knew that a fraternal code for sport angling would be viable only for true anglers; for all others, regulatory controls were the necessary strategy to employ. In some way, the sport code adopted in the hearts of the informal company of anglers required codification in law, and Roosevelt was admirably equipped to carry the flag. Extremely perceptive and environmentally wise, Roosevelt supported the enactment of consistent laws to protect wildlife in every state. He argued that because the habits of freshwater fish were well known, it was possible and necessary to provide consistent and uniform protection across the states during the spawning season. Otherwise differing laws would create loopholes by which fish could be killed in one state and sold in another (74).

Robert Roosevelt felt that blame for injury to game fell not as much on a lack of new laws as the lack of enforcing existing laws. He was of the opinion that enforcement was a primary duty of angling clubs and individual anglers, who owed it to themselves and to the wild creatures. Roosevelt maintained, "Wanton injury to public property, in game, should be punished precisely as similar injury to public property in grounds or buildings, by incarcerating the offender in prison; for of the two, the latter is less injurious in its ultimate results" (74).

None of the Roosevelt family members were timid. Robert's nephew, Theodore "Teddy" Roosevelt, definitely took lessons from his uncle on this topic and used them to his benefit when he was president of the United States. On October 28, 1903, in response to his request, President Roosevelt received a letter from the Department of the Interior stating that action was being taken for "forest rangers to [also] become state game wardens to enforce game laws (95)"—an action I believe his Uncle Robert would have praised.

Commercial fish harvesting activities in the northern section of the country earned Robert Roosevelt's anger when reports surfaced that fishing nets with meshes small enough to catch yearling trout were in common use. Worse, the young trout were frequently thrown aside and left to die. Each winter, net fishing caught thousands of large fish in the act of spawning or shortly thereafter; consequently, millions of unborn trout were irrevocably lost. Fittingly, Roosevelt advocated that sport anglers and hunters have a responsibility to protect game because they have the greatest at stake. He encouraged sport-minded individuals to discourage, by their conversation and example, all violations of the law and any inhumane or wasteful actions of what should be sport. Beyond that, he stated that if an obvious infraction were observed, the individuals responsible for the destruction of the wildlife should be exposed and shunned, and further action would be taken to pursue the enactment of enlightened statutes (74).

Robert Roosevelt also advocated the elimination of hunting fish by gigging, the most lethal form of spearing. A gig is a spear with a multipronged, barbed head. By use of these tools, many eastern streams lost every animal that swam: not only the trout but also the catfish, eels, suckers, and frogs. In some locales gigging, primarily an evening activity, was a pastime popularly engaged in by young boys. Many states eventually outlawed gigging, but some continue to allow the practice, mostly for certain nuisance species for which traditional angling methods are ineffective.

Roosevelt began his conservation work in his home state of New York by founding the New York State Fishery Commission in 1867. Without salary, he served there as a fish commissioner from 1868 to 1888. The annual reports of the commission, prepared chiefly by him personally, led to the appointment of similar commissions in other states. He continued his conservation efforts on a national level as a member of Congress from New York's Fourth Congressional District. He initiated the bill creating the US Fish Commission, established by a joint resolution of Congress on February 9, 1871. That commission was the predecessor of the US Fish and Wildlife Service and its fisheries program.

> Act of Feb. 9, 1871, Sess. III, Res. 22, Stat. 593–94 (1871)
> Forty-First Congress. SESS. III. RES. 18, 19, 20, 21, 22.
> 1871. 563
> Joint Resolution for the Protection and Preservation of the
> Food Fishes of the Coast of the United States.

> Whereas it is asserted that the most valuable food fishes of the coast and the lakes of the United States are rapidly diminishing in number, to the public injury, and so as materially to affect the interests of trade and commerce: Therefore, Be it resolved... That the President be, and he hereby is, authorized and required to appoint... one person of proved scientific and practical acquaintance with the fishes... to be commissioner of fish and fisheries.... It shall be the duty of said commissioner to prosecute

investigations and inquiries on the subject, with the view
of ascertaining whether any and what diminution in the
number of the food fishes of the coast and the lakes of the
United States has taken place; and, if so, to what causes
the same is due; and also whether any and what protective,
prohibitory, or precautionary measures should be adopted in the premises.... The heads of the executive depart-
ments... are hereby, directed to cause to be rendered all
necessary and practicable aid to the said commissioner
in the prosecution of the investigations and inquiries....
It shall be lawful for said commissioner to take, or cause
to be taken, at all times... in the waters of the lakes, such
fish or specimens... needful... for the conduct of his duties...
any law, custom, or usage of any State to the contrary
notwithstanding.

The modern fisheries program focuses on high-priority fish species and
habitats that protect and preserve stable fish populations and healthy
habitats. This is accomplished across America via "a network of dedicated professionals engaged in their craft at 72 National Fish Hatcheries, 65
Fish and Wildlife Conservation Offices, a Historic National Fish Hatchery,
9 Fish Health Centers, 7 Fish Technology Centers, and the Aquatic Animal
Drug Approval Partnership" (96).

Roosevelt influenced his young nephew Theodore to become a conserva-
tionist. As a result, Theodore desired to be a naturalist, a scientist examining nature. As president, Theodore Roosevelt never forgot the love of
nature originally instilled in his heart by his uncle Robert. He successfully preserved vast regions of the United States for future generations
of Americans. At this writing, all fifty states and the District of Columbia
regulate fishing, and all require a license to fish. Many states have fishing
laws that apply throughout the state, while others have different laws for
different bodies of water. Both the fish and the angling community owe
a lot to the significant contributions of Robert Barnwell Roosevelt.

# Angling Method: High Sport or Humble

Nineteenth-century angling authors, discussing qualities that constitute a true sport angler, often argued over the angling method: fly-fishing versus bait angling. In fact, Robert Roosevelt stated, "Therefore to his many other qualities, the true sportsman must add a thorough knowledge of fly-fishing." Roosevelt obviously considered fly-fishing the epitome of sport fishing, and he developed an order of precedence for game fish (commonly accepted during the period). The three fish at the top of Roosevelt's order—salmon, trout, and black bass—would all take the fly. Interestingly, the pike, muskellunge, and walleye were omitted, along with others that he certainly angled for and addressed in other pages of his book *Superior Fishing*.

Regardless of Roosevelt's opinions, the debate on angling methods continued. During the early days of the twentieth century—the heyday of the too-short baitcasting rod and the heavy, hook-laden wooden plug-style lure—baitcasters took a lot of heat for the lack of sport they exhibited. Even beyond the mid-twentieth century, some believed modern baitcasting to be the humbler brother's sport. Goodspeed, the angling historian, wrote in his 1939 book *Angling in America*, "Bait-casting was, and perhaps is now except when fly-fishing for bass is practiced, the commoner mode of fishing in our middle states" (5).

Many of today's anglers realize how varied and individually adaptable baitcasting has become since the early days in Kentucky. It continues to meet the needs of many thousands of individual baitcasters, many of whom, I suspect, spend little time considering which method of angling is at a higher level of sport. Each of the nineteenth-century authors referenced in this chapter used multiple angling methods, as do many sport-minded twenty-first-century individuals. Associating certain angling methods with certain social classes was, and remains, a ridiculous endeavor that modern Americans should be well past. Many novice anglers began with a spincasting reel, still-fishing with worms and bobbers; some have faithfully remained with that equipment and technique throughout their days. In fortunate moments, they proudly and happily land what they believe is a nice fish; angling just made their day a little nicer. Angling practiced lawfully, honorably, and with enjoyment is true angling. Fittingly, Thaddeus Norris, brilliantly drawing on four famous words of Sir Henry Wotton, said, "The true angler... With him, fishing is a recreation and a 'calmer of unquiet thoughts'" (68).

Robert B. Roosevelt

(Courtesy of the Library of Congress)

## Chapter 8
# EVOLUTION OF THE SHORT BAITCASTING ROD

*1885 to 1920*

## The Baitcasting System

Accomplished twenty-first-century anglers often think in terms of a baitcasting system—a properly balanced rod, reel, line, and lures assembled to achieve certain desired results. The foundation of the system, the rod, is selected first, because it must fit the kind of fishing intended. The reel is chosen by how it fits the rod, the amount of line it must hold, and the drag system employed. Next, the line is matched to the rod and reel, taking into consideration its weight, diameter, and material. Lastly, lures are selected to complement all of the foregoing.

The objective of this chapter is to reveal the history of the "short" baitcasting rod, a rod form responsible for much of the early growth of the sport. Prior to World War I, the components of the baitcasting system did not necessarily evolve together in harmony; therefore, balancing certain combinations of constituent parts became an art rather than mere equipment selection.

In Kentucky during the early to mid-nineteenth century, anglers used live bait and a still-fishing technique. The standard equipment for the affluent Bluegrass anglers consisted of a Kentucky multiplying reel, usually lashed onto a supple ten- to twelve-foot top section of native cane rod (once common in the Southeastern states) with affixed standing line guides. The angler deployed a minnow with a sweeping, one-handed sidearm cast. This easy, graceful movement allowed live minnows, typically hooked through the lips, to remain undamaged. Dr. Henshall angled with just such a setup when he practiced medicine in Cynthiana, Kentucky, during the Civil War. By the early 1870s the single-piece cane rod was improved by fastening an upper 6½-foot portion of cane to a tapered wooden butt about twenty inches long. This provided a better-balanced rod (not top-heavy) with a stronger, easier-to-use handle.

# The Henshall Rod

In an article titled "The Coming Black Bass Rod" in the February 1875 edition of *Forest and Stream* magazine, Henshall announced a new type of fishing rod that he had produced for his own use. The rod described was in three sections, each 34½ inches long; when fully assembled it measured 8 feet 3 inches long and weighed 8 ounces. Subsequently Henshall engaged Abbey & Imbrie of New York to produce a professionally made version of the rod to his specifications, and he was elated with the results. In his 1881 *Book of the Black Bass* Henshall discussed the new rod, and in his 1889 book, *More About the Black Bass,* he provided additional detail and clarification. By then, most of the finest American rod manufactures were producing Henshall's rod, and it became the standard for baitcasting through the end of the nineteenth century.

## Chicago: A Largemouth Bass–Fishing Town

Emerson Hough, one of the most successful writers of nonfiction accounts of the American West, related that at the turn of the twentieth century, Chicago was a largemouth bass–fishing town with an unfortunate landscape not conducive to shore fishing. Hough's article "Angling in the Middle West," published in the August 1901 issue of *Outing* magazine, described Chicago bass angling as happening in bright, shallow lakes with mud-fringed shorelines and beds of bulrushes extending twenty or more yards into the water, making fishing difficult for those without a boat. He said it was in this shallow water that largemouth bass hunted for frogs among the tangled roots and weeds under the lily pads. The clear water proved yet another impediment: bass could see the angler even at distances of ten yards or more (97).

Hough, later manager of the Chicago branch of *Field & Stream*, defined the problem of the Chicago baitcaster: "how to stand away some twenty-five or thirty yards from the feeding ground of the bass and yet be able to deliver the frog with accuracy into the little pockets or open places among the lilies and rushes. Moreover, it was necessary to snail that bass out from the entangling weeds into the open water after he had struck and gorged the frog" (97).

# The Problem Was the Long Rod

Earlier it was noted that to increase the chances of a catch, Kentucky anglers needed to present a baited hook across a large area of water, an issue solved by George Snyder's reel. In Chicago, anglers loved the Kentucky reel: it was the perfect tool to perform the long cast required. The problem was the rod. Bass rods made to Henshall's specifications were overly long with a flexible temperament. Casting with them required a sweeping underhand motion, starting at a point below the elbow and ending at a point about face level. The rod was ineffective in Chicago, where anglers needed a tool capable of casting heavy bait weighing two ounces or more, like frogs, for significant distances while also being strong enough to extract bass from the weeds. Hough's historical account, published in a 1901 article, disclosed how the typical Chicago angler solved the problem.

> He shortened his rod to eight feet, then to seven feet eight, then to seven feet six. Then he cut off something of the butt below the reel and got his rod down to seven feet. A few have even gone below that, and to this day the six-foot split bamboo casting rod is not an uncommon thing.... It is too stiff to give much sport.... It has just enough spring at the top to make it a perfect catapult for throwing frogs (97).

Herbert Grissom, a refined baitcaster, described this shortened rod in a 1915 article: "In its first crude form the short rod was nothing more than a stiff, stout stick with a hand-grasp and reel-seat at one end, and was designed to facilitate casting... using heavy baits" (98).

Henshall's reaction to the rod, although somewhat harsh, is consistent with that of some other sport-minded individuals in the eastern states. A person of the highest integrity and always the consummate sportsman, Henshall championed the bass. As both an avid fly-fisher and baitcaster, Henshall played the game as a "gentle art" with a "just appreciation of the amenities." His tackle, and the skill, judgment, and precision in which he deployed it, expressed this. Commenting on the short rod in his final edition of *Book of the Black Bass*, under the heading "The Frog-Casting Rod," Henshall wrote:

> Rods—we must call them so by courtesy—are now made... for casting... overhead and forward.... It has its advantages; for the rod being not only very short, but very stiff, the fish can be reeled rapidly to the landing net. This mode of

angling however does not appeal to one who has... a love
for suitable tackle or to one who, being imbued with the
proper *esprit de corps*, is disposed to give the fish a chance
(99).

Henshall's opinion initially left the Chicago anglers with a conundrum:
use a short, stiff frog-casting rod or live with a clear conscience. At the end
of the day, the short rod did not go away; rather, its popularity soared for
the reason Henshall himself noted. In fact, moves were afoot to shorten
the rod even more.

## J. M. Clarke and Fred D. Devine

The origin of the short rod, specifically designed to cast live frogs, actually
preceded Henshall's published concerns by more than two decades. In
1885 Fred D. Divine, a rod maker in Utica, New York, produced the first
example of the new rod designed by his Chicago client, J. M. Clarke, a
local angler and tournament baitcaster. Clarke was also a charter member
of the Chicago Fly Casting Club along with his longtime colleague,
Emerson Hough (100).

Given Hough's lengthy personal association with Clarke, his professional
experience documenting events, and the exacting detail he used in
recording the short rod's development, I believe that Hough's 1901 article
describes some of the calculated actions Clarke himself undertook to
develop the specifications required by Fred Divine to build the new rod.
Did Clarke also develop the now famous overhead cast necessary to use
the rod? The possibility exists. However, it is more probable that the
overhead cast that we have come to know developed as a collective
effort by Chicago's fraternity of largemouth bass anglers who had
angled together for many years.

Although he did not mention the overhead cast, Clarke provided the
following information in response to a letter asking about the rod.

> The first conception of the Short Bait Casting rod was made
> for me in 1885 by Fred D. Divine, now the Fred D. Divine
> Company, of Utica, New York. The rod was made out of
> lancewood, 6 feet, 3 inches long. The rod was a revelation
> in those days, as the usual lengths of rods was 10½ feet.
> I fought the point and won out. To-day my banner rod is
> 5 feet, 6 inches (101).

Clarke, a successful tournament caster since 1892, placed second as an amateur at the Chicago tournament on September 21, 1893. As a prize, he received a Bethabara wood baitcasting rod with German silver trimmings and agate guides, valued at twenty-five dollars. It had been donated by Fred D. Divine, the maker of Clarke's original short rod and a tournament caster. Divine's participation at the tournament is not surprising, because the sport provided a worthwhile forum for introducing new rods, reels, and other tackle, and Divine was well known as an avid participant. Tragically, Divine, the master rod maker, sustained fatal injuries as the result of a horrendous accident in his Utica manufacturing plant on March 16, 1900; he died within hours.

Fittingly, Fred D. Divine's company, operated after his death by his wife, figured prominently at the September 17, 1904, tournament sponsored by the Chicago Fly Casting Club in Garfield Park on Chicago's West Side. Of the thirty-eight competitors participating in the baitcasting long distance event and distance and accuracy event in the ½-ounce weight class, ten of them used Divine-made rods. The longest of the Divine rods was 6 feet, 8½ inches; the shortest was 5½ feet. In fact, the statistics for these events indicate that of the rods used, 77 percent (29 rods) were longer than six feet; 18 percent (7 rods) were between five and six feet; and 5 percent (2 rods) were shorter than five feet. The difference in size between the longest rod (6 feet, 8½ inches) and the shortest, made by Racine (4 feet, 6½ inches) illustrates that the phrase "short rod" is a relative term.

## The Ideal Short Rod and Lesser Others

The rods employed in the tournament casting events were the most well-built, well-balanced rods available. In his highly noteworthy defense of the short rod in his *Outing* magazine article "The Black Bass and Some Sportsman," Herbert Grissom described an ideal short rod.

> It is a fairy wand; it is a thing of life, as wonderfully delicate and strong and truly balanced as the best of fly-rods... built of bamboo by master hands... Its action is supple, empathetic and lightning fast (98).

It appears that a rod capable of becoming the foundation of a balanced baitcasting system came at a high price, because Grissom said they cost from fifteen to sixty dollars and were worth it (98). Grissom also disclosed a dark truth: the tournament rods were not in the least representative of the vast majority of short rods used by everyday baitcasters.

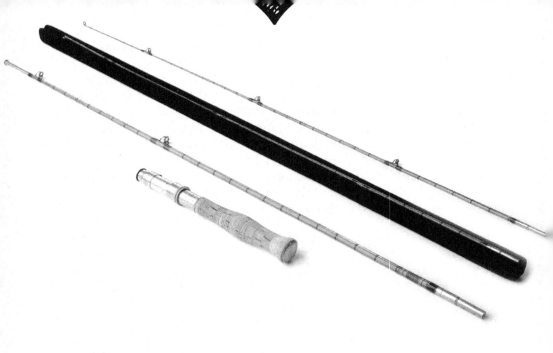

The Fairy Wand: H. Leonard rod, six feet long with two rod tips

In response to a *Saturday Evening Post* contributor's allegation that the short rod was a "stick and not a rod" and therefore a less sporting tool, Grissom said, "Unhappily, the description is only too accurate in a majority of cases. The vastly greater numbers of the short casting rods now on the market are sticks or clubs built of bamboo, solid wood, or steel, varying in length from three to six feet and wholly unfit for sportsmanlike angling" (98). Besides being stiff, another reason those rods were unfit is that rods fewer than five feet long did not have the action (functionality) required to allow use of the most accurate casting technique—the overhead cast. In his book *Black Bass Fishing: Theory and Practice*, Robert Page Lincoln, one of the most highly respected anglers of the first half of the twentieth century, addressed the principal limitations of the stiff, too-short rod.

> These short rods were first, last and all the time meant for side casting; and side casting, as it was carried on, was at best a chuck-and-chance-method. It remained for the 5½-foot rod to usher in the overhead cast.... The rod must possess some degree of resiliency to aid in projecting the lure to destination.... It is impossible to manage the overhead cast with a short rod. It can be done with a 5½-foot rod, but less well with a 5-foot rod. (102).

# Casting Tournaments Promote Rod Development

The casting tournaments performed an important function as a development and testing laboratory for the fishing tackle industry (100), and tackle manufacturers in general took a participative interest. William Shakespeare Jr. of Kalamazoo, Michigan—eponymous founder of the famous tackle company—occasionally participated as a contestant and was closely associated with the casters. In 1902 Shakespeare was the guest of honor at the tournament in Grand Rapids, Michigan, where he participated as a contestant in the accuracy bait event (103). Shakespeare's 1902 tackle catalog included a pamphlet entitled "The Art of Bait-Casting," which proclaimed:

> The tackle required for bait casting is... a short rod, a quadruple-multiplying reel, a fine line, and one or more artificial baits.... As the result of the most careful and exhaustive tests, a rod 5-½-feet long has been found capable of making the longest and most accurate casts, and at the same time being the most satisfactory for steady and continuous fishing (104).

By 1905 Shakespeare was specializing in tournament casting rods. The sport of competition casting gave Shakespeare an excellent way to capitalize on this new focus and enter a market previously dominated by other manufacturers. Shakespeare ramped up an advertising campaign and found a champion, Lloyd J. Tooley, a tournament caster and owner of Tooley Tackle Company of Detroit, Michigan. A member of the local Kalamazoo Casting Club, Tooley appeared in Shakespeare's advertisements during 1905, when he set the world distance casting record of 194 feet, 8 inches using a ½-ounce weight with a four-foot, ten-inch Shakespeare short rod (100).

## Lightweight ¼-Ounce Lures and Tournament Weights

Two years later, in 1907, the National Association of Scientific Angling Clubs (NASAC) supplemented the tournament competition events by adding a new ¼-ounce weight classification. The impetus for using lighter weight undoubtedly came from sport-minded individuals like William Jamison, a Chicago tackle manufacturer.

Exceptionally proficient at casting lightweight tackle, Jamison was the 1907 professional tournament champion in both the ¼-ounce and ½-ounce classes in the accuracy category; later the same year he won the first American Bass Tournament. Jamison's light tackle prowess required the use of a balanced baitcasting system and the expertise to operate it at maximum potential. In 1907 a finely balanced baitcasting system could cost seventy-five to a hundred dollars—the equivalent of two months' wages for the average American—and acquiring the expertise to cast with it cost hundreds of hours of practice. Grissom agreed that mastering the art of casting is difficult, saying that "many are called... few are chosen.... That is why the landscape is cluttered up with atrocious short rod casters" (98).

According to Lou S. Darling in his 1907 book *Tournament Casting and the Proper Equipment* (105), rods for the ½-ounce weight class were fairly short and stiff. Darling's own rod was 5½ feet long. He maintained that rods of this type "should have a quick, snappy action... a short, sharp drive and at the finish of the movement should spring back immediately and remain rigid and not quiver and vibrate." Regarding the lighter weight, Darling said, "For the ¼-ounce and accuracy events the rod should be a little longer and more pliable, for the caster, on account of the lighter weight in use, has to depend more on the spring of the rod."

## Effect of Reel Spool Weight

Regarding the reel, Darling noted that two schools of thought existed. One supported using a heavy spool and crank handle to maximize momentum so as to keep the spool running and "feed line without dragging back against the casting weight." The other "insists upon the lightest possible form of construction for spool and handle" to reduce inertia for a quicker start. Passage of time settles most arguments, so it is interesting to see how seventeen years later, in 1924, Fred Arbogast, famous tackle manufacturer and renowned world champion tournament caster, provided additional input.

> The principle of using a longer[,] more flexible rod to cast light [lures] and a shorter, stiffer rod for a heavy weight is old, but the more important theory of using a lighter spooled reel for casting a light weight and a heavier spooled reel for a heavy weight has not received much publicity (106).

Arbogast first pointed out the correlation between the length and action of the casting rod and the weight it is able to cast, then settled the question of spool weight. When casting ½-ounce lures, Arbogast used a reel having a spool weight of 30 grams. For casting ¼-ounce lures, he switched to aluminum line spool heads to decrease spool weight to 20 grams.

In 1907 Kentucky reels with lightweight reel spools could be had; no doubt, tournament casters like Jamison enjoyed such features, just as Arbogast did. Generally, however, average anglers on a budget could not afford them. This being the case, what opportunities might exist for the novice angler of modest means to deploy lightweight tackle? Unfortunately, the answer is that it would be difficult to do so without a lighter reel spool. Nonetheless, other ungainly options were under consideration.

John B. Thompson, writing as Ozark Ripley, pointed out that the tackle manufacturers were responsible for growing the sport of baitcasting. They "exploited bait casting in all the outdoor magazines to such a vast extent that they sold the sport of bait casting and bait casting products to hundreds of thousands of anglers" (107). Thompson asserted that when baitcasting became popular, more changes in rods were seen. "They became still shorter... due to the obvious presence of heavy lures" (107).

## Heddon Promotes Short Rods and Heavy Lures

In 1907, casting lighter lures (½ ounce or less) required longer, more supple rods of approximately 5½ feet in length and lightweight reel spools that were not generally available to the crowds of novice baitcasters. The typical novice cast using a heavy-spooled reel without a level wind or backlash control. These were readily available from the Sears and Roebuck catalog; prices for their celebrated quadruple multiplying model ranged from less than a dollar to three dollars, depending on the materials used.

James Heddon & Son, the famous tackle manufacturers from Dowagiac, Michigan, published an article titled "The Art of Bait Casting" in their 1906 and 1907 catalogs. In the article, Heddon advised that the short rod of 4½ feet to 4 feet, 10 inches is the perfect size for casting the popular weights of modern artificial lures. The article asserted that heavier lures were becoming more popular each year because of varied and adverse wind conditions that detracted from distance and accuracy when using the regulation ½-ounce tournament lure weight. Consequently, the very short rod would be best suited.

At face value, this seems a dubious, thinly-veiled argument. What would precipitate such a contention? Certainly a slightly longer rod would cast a ½-ounce lure with more ease than a short, stiff one, and a rod of the type Heddon advocated would never be able to cast the ¼-ounce lure. Also important is that a rod as short as 4½ feet would require using a less accurate side-arm cast (102). Heddon seemed disconnected from the sport of tournament casting, and I wondered why.

Lures cataloged by James Heddon & Son between 1902 and 1907 were hook-laden, heavy lures weighing ¾ ounces and more. However, the company did offer two lighter ½-ounce lures, both exquisitely detailed and of very high quality: the Artistic Minnow and the Dowagiac Minnow No. 20, which was available by 1909. The Artistic Minnow measured 1¾ inches, employed a single trailing treble hook, weighed ½ ounce, and came with an attachment, the purpose of which is recorded in the catalog.

> This Minnow will appeal especially to those anglers who object to the multiplicity of hooks on the other Minnows. It is regulation casting weight. viz, ½ ounce, and an extra attachment comes with each Minnow to give additional casting weight if desired.

Heddon Artistic Minnow with Attachment

The attachment took the form of a ¼-ounce, oblong wooden float that, in general shape, resembled the lure body. Painted the color of lead, it was capable of being affixed to the line about three inches forward of the lure. It actually had two functions: the additional buoyancy of the wood kept the lure higher off the lake bottom, and the extra ¼ ounce of weight brought the lure to a heftier ¾ ounce. The extra weight aided in casting with a short, heavy rod. Collectors refer to the rarely found and highly valued attachment as a "weight-buoy." By 1910, both the Artistic Minnow and the Dowagiac Minnow had disappeared from Heddon's catalog. My conclusion is that they were too lightweight for the short, side-arm casting rods advocated by Heddon.

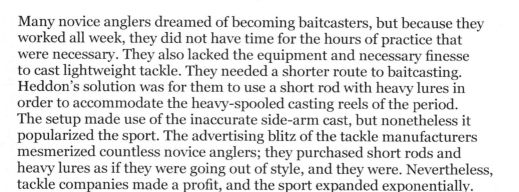

Many novice anglers dreamed of becoming baitcasters, but because they worked all week, they did not have time for the hours of practice that were necessary. They also lacked the equipment and necessary finesse to cast lightweight tackle. They needed a shorter route to baitcasting. Heddon's solution was for them to use a short rod with heavy lures in order to accommodate the heavy-spooled casting reels of the period. The setup made use of the inaccurate side-arm cast, but nonetheless it popularized the sport. The advertising blitz of the tackle manufacturers mesmerized countless novice anglers; they purchased short rods and heavy lures as if they were going out of style, and they were. Nevertheless, tackle companies made a profit, and the sport expanded exponentially.

## Untutored Anglers

Unfortunately, many of the new anglers that swelled the number of baitcasters became scapegoats of the sport. For a time, many ignored the deficiency in accuracy of the side-arm casting technique—they still caught fish, so why change? The unfortunate downside is that short rods changed how many new adherents played the game. Inexperienced novices using unsporting equipment while ignorant of conservation became formidable killers of unwary fish. To know this is true, a person has only to view early twentieth-century photographs showing anglers holding stringers with more fish than any family of ten could reasonably eat or keep from rotting in the days before freezers. In his 1937 book *How to Catch Game Fish*, Jack Lamb, one of the premier bass anglers in America with thirty-five thousand recorded instances of catch and release from 1920 to 1935, recounted that in the early days of baitcasting (circa 1900–1915), fly casters "looked with disdain upon the plug caster" (108)—a reasonable perspective considering the practices of some untutored anglers.

As well as catapulting frogs, the short rod catapulted the sport into the modern age of baitcasting. Just as the 1875 demarcation point between the Smith Age and Golden Age of tackle manufacturing represents an approximate transition date from one age to another, the same logic applies here. The early age of baitcasting began with the production of Snyder's first reel; it continued through the transformation from still-fishing to the birth of baitcasting as a new sport in 1881 and its subsequent growth through the remainder of the nineteenth century. The modern age began in 1900, when broad segments of the population became adherents of the sport.

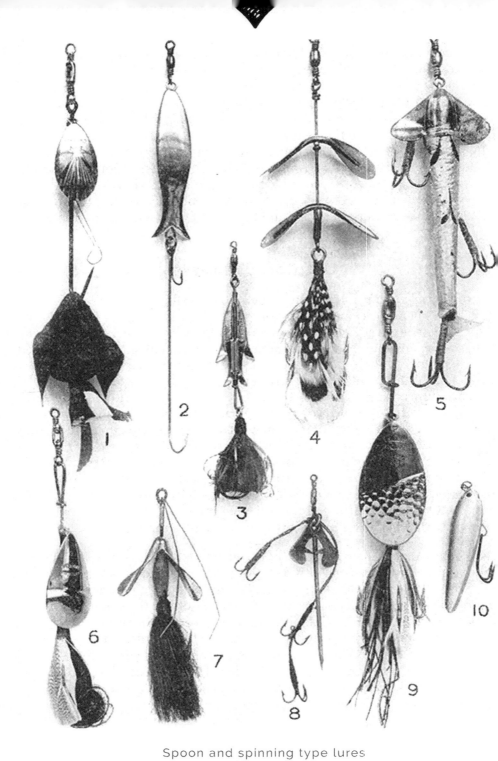

Spoon and spinning type lures

(From the book Fishing, Tackle and Kits by Dixie Carroll)

# Chapter 9

# NOTEWORTHY BAITCASTING LURES

*1883 to 1935*

## The First Plugs

During the mid-nineteenth century, the availability of artificial casting lures other than the variations of spoons and spinners was sparse. It is true that various English baits—such as the Phantom, usually made from a combination of metal and fabric—were available. Even American inventions, like Riley Haskell's brass and copper trolling minnow, although rarely found, did exist. However, the hard-bodied wooden casting lures so familiar fifty years later, called "plugs" (so named for their cylindrical shape, like the plug of a wooden barrel), were virtually nonexistent. I have sometimes wondered who made the first of them and when.

The last quarter of the nineteenth century produced what numerous individuals consider to be the first artificial wooden lure: Harry Comstock's Flying Hellgrammite, patented January 30, 1883, in New York. This classic, with a 2½-inch-long wooden body, employs a set of large nickel-plated metal wings just shy of two inches long. However, it is an imitation of the Eastern Dobsonfly and therefore is technically not a plug.

A second contender for the honor of the earliest plug lure comes from comments made by a highly reputable individual: J. M. Clarke, the tournament caster who designed the archetypal short rod produced by Fred Divine in 1885. Clarke, highly respected and well known for many years in the sports trade business, was definitely in a position to know when new lures hit the market. According to a 1918 article by Sam S. Stinson in *The American Angler*, Clarke believed the first commercially produced plug was Charles Shaffer's lure, advertised as the Woods Expert Minnow, introduced commercially around 1885. Clarke recalled that it was a success from the start (109). However, other than Clarke's statement, no documentation yet exists that Shaffer's lure was the earliest plug produced.

# A Heddon Story

In recognition of the above information, it appears appropriate to now consider the legendary story of how James Heddon came to create his wooden frog lure, often regarded as the first wooden casting lure. The classic story involves Heddon tossing a small piece of carved wood into the water, a bass striking it, and Heddon spawning an idea for a wooden fish lure.

A different account was told by James Heddon's oldest son, William(Will), to an interviewer from the *Clermont Press* in Florida in 1927, when Will was fifty-seven years old. Will said that as far as he knew, Charlie Harris, a conductor on the Michigan Central Railroad, made the first artificial lure about twenty-seven years before the interview, or circa 1900. It was made of cork with a hook on each leg and a gang hook dangling from the belly. Frank Peak came to Dowagiac with a Harris frog lure and presented it to James Harley, whom Peak taught to cast. In turn, Harley introduced his friend James Heddon to baitcasting using Harris's frog. Later, Heddon carved out his own wooden frog somewhat slimmer than the Harris bait, and it proved better for keeping fish hooked. It featured gang hooks on the front and a bottle cap to produce a water spray, a technique well known to fly-casters. Soon Heddon's friends were asking him to make additional frogs.

As for which of the various contenders deserves the title of inventor of the wooden plug lure, I will not venture a guess. However, within a very short time following its invention, a plethora of wooden lures in all colors and shapes were available to entice the fast-growing crowd of baitcasters. Immediately prior to the turn of the twentieth century, manufacturers like James Heddon were already designing lures and manufacturing processes and producing lures in their family homes.

# The First Mass-Produced Plug

James Heddon, the innovator, knew that wooden lures would eventually transition into various forms. In 1902 the James Heddon & Son company produced three different plug-type lures. These early hard-bodied wooden lures came in two types:

- Surface lures that floated continuously on the water: the Dowagiac Expert Perfect Surface Casting Bait (two treble hooks) and the Dowagiac No. 2 (four treble hooks).

- An underwater lure that sank and remained submerged until retrieved to the surface: the Dowagiac Underwater.

Heddon's first product, the Dowagiac Expert, holds a special place in the evolution of lures because it is generally recognized as the first mass-produced wooden plug. US Patent 696,433, awarded to James Heddon on April 1, 1902, applied to the Expert and to each of the other two Heddon lures produced at that time. The patent addressed four aspects of the lure: the collar positioned around the lure's nose end; the inward-tapered cavity, or socket, holding the hook hardware; the open screw eye for fastening the hook to the lure body; and the sloped nose end (but only when used in combination with the aforementioned collar).

The Expert differed from the patent drawing in that it used only two treble hooks: one hanging from the center of the belly, slightly forward of the placement of the "E" hook shown in the drawing, and one in the tail position "C."

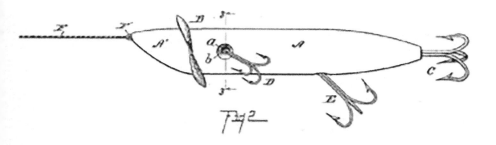

Drawing from US Patent 696,433

The Expert was painted white and sold for seventy-five cents. The first hook fastened under the belly with a screw-eye fastener inserted into a cylindrical, inward-tapered cavity that lacked a metal cup insert, the purpose being to keep the hooks away from the lure body and therefore better aligned to catch fish. The second treble hook, attached to the end of the tail by a screw-eye fastener, employed a brass external tail cup. A circular collar was fastened to the fore end of the lure to create a spray of water in order to attract fish. The catalog does not list the lure length or weight; however, collectors report it to be 4½ inches long.

By 1903 James Heddon & Son recognized the importance of developing and testing new lures. Will Heddon and his wife Laura began "combining business with pleasure" at Fort Pierce, Florida. There they tested the first Heddon lure, the Dowagiac Expert, which their boatman referred to as the "white thing" (110). Quickly thereafter, they established a headquarters for lure development in a boathouse at the Jolly Palms Resort on Plum Lake, just east of Lake Minneola, part of Florida's Palatlakaha lake chain and river (111).

# Noteworthy Innovative Lures

As lure development and innovation occurred at Heddon's Florida center, it also happened at many other locations throughout the country. Soon Heddon's competitors offered new forms of lures in a staggering number of choices, with additional functionality (actual or claimed) beyond those offered by Heddon. Some, the old proverb tells us, would catch only anglers and not fish. In contrast, other lures would, like Heddon's Expert, stand out as somehow being significant for improving the functionality of the baitcasting system generally. These lures include:

- William Jamison's Coaxer, winner of the first American bass tournament and archetype of the upturned hook lure.

- Shannon's Twin Spinner, archetype of spinner baits.

- The Creek Chub Bait Company's No. 100 Wiggler, archetype of floater/diver crankbaits.

- Nick and Cosma Creme's Wiggle Worm, archetype of soft plastic worm baits.

- Lauri Rapala's Original Floating Wobbler, contender for top fish producer.

Each of these lures has remarkable features that advanced the performance of the baitcasting system. Four of the five lures are the archetype of their respective lure type, and the remaining lure is arguably the most productive lure ever produced.

*William Jamison's Coaxer (1907)*

Coaxer

Before artificial baitcasting lures attained general popularity, natural baits such as minnows, frogs, and worms were often replaced by a chunk of pork rind cut into a two- inch-long triangular shape, with about half an inch of pork fat still attached to the skin. A weedless, upturned hook was inserted at the forward tip of the rind, and the lure was deployed using a skittering technique to move it over lily pads and other obstructions. This lure was highly effective for bass and pike.

In 1907 William Jamison (the tackle manufacturer and champion caster discussed in Chapter 8) took the pork lure a step further. While competing in the Sixth Scientific Angling Tournament—where he won the baitcasting accuracy events in both the ¼-ounce and ½-ounce weight classes (100)—Jamison was, as always, on the lookout for good ideas to catch fish. He observed another angler decorating an old-style pork chunk with a piece of red yarn and noted that it appeared to increase the number of bass strikes. Jamison decided to advance the idea somewhat by actually inserting the yarn underneath the rind while also leaving a length of yarn long enough to trail behind the chunk as it skittered through the water. His innovation worked, and soon other anglers who observed his efforts started to follow suit. Jamison continued to evolve his idea by swapping the pork chunk with a glossy white painted cork body, replacing the yarn with a red feather tail (109), and adding a small red felt wing on each side. Armed with a single upturned hook, it made a great lure for fishing weedy water, and the artificial quality was preferable to dealing with pork fat. Jamison named the new lure "Coaxer."

Interestingly, another account of the Coaxer lure was written by Jamison's competitor, James Heddon, while angling in Florida. Heddon said, "I have a lure in my tackle box, going under the title of 'the Coaxer,' that was copied from a chunk of pork—at one time quite popular with Chicago bait casters.... It's a nice bait.... Where nothing but turned up hooks can be used... this is a very good lure" (112).

In 1910, Jamison's confidence in the Coaxer's ability to attract fish and entice them to strike inspired him to issue a public fishing contest challenge in *Field & Stream* magazine: "I offer to meet any angler on earth, manufacturers of artificial baits preferred, in a three-day fishing contest, on any lake within 500 miles of Chicago to prove that the sportsmanlike Coaxer, with its humane armament, will actually catch more fish than any other bait on the market, or the live frog or minnow." This contest, which took place in Hartville, Ohio, became the first bass tournament in recorded history.

Having previous experience with the Coaxer and knowing Jamison's world-class proficiency may have given James and Will Heddon second thoughts, as they did not take up the challenge; but another angler did.

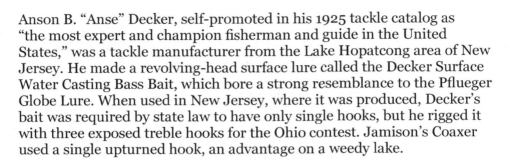

Anson B. "Anse" Decker, self-promoted in his 1925 tackle catalog as "the most expert and champion fisherman and guide in the United States," was a tackle manufacturer from the Lake Hopatcong area of New Jersey. He made a revolving-head surface lure called the Decker Surface Water Casting Bass Bait, which bore a strong resemblance to the Pflueger Globe Lure. When used in New Jersey, where it was produced, Decker's bait was required by state law to have only single hooks, but he rigged it with three exposed treble hooks for the Ohio contest. Jamison's Coaxer used a single upturned hook, an advantage on a weedy lake.

The two men—along with Bill Macy, representing *Field & Stream* magazine, and two other judges—met on Congress Lake, a small, weedy private lake not known for being overly productive. On June 16, 1910, the angling commenced. The contestants fished for three days from the same boat with an oarsman in between them. Jamison easily won the contest because the Coaxer was able to penetrate the lily pads where the bass were located; his opponent, relegated to fishing the outer edges, angled in less fertile water. At the end of the third day, the score was twenty-eight bass for Jamison, sixteen for Decker.

The eyes of the angling nation were on this contest, described with scientific objectivity by *Field & Stream*, the contest's sponsor. According to A. J. McClane, executive editor at *Field & Stream* until 1977, "This Armageddon of the weed beds resolved nothing" (113). The contentious debate over lures ran on with no end in sight, but both Decker and Jamison reaped great rewards from the contest in the form of promotional value and boasting rights. The Coaxer was, according to Robert Page Lincoln, the first lure to use the upturned single hook and one of the most successful surface lures in the early days of baitcasting (102). The Coaxer is the first of its kind and therefore the archetype of the upturned hook lure.

*Shannon's Twin Spinner (1916)*

Twin Spinner

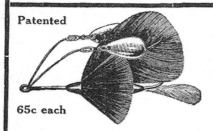

Jesse P. Shannon of Geneva, Wisconsin, designed the archetype of spinner baits, the Shannon Twin Spinner. The 1916 patent application made it a centenarian in 2016. Shannon was awarded US Patent 1,295,617 on February 25, 1919; but before that, around 1917, he had relinquished those rights to William Jamison. The W. J. Jamison Company at 5559 W. North Ave., Chicago, produced the lure for many years. By the 1960s the company had transitioned into the Shannon Tackle Corporation, located at 3654 W. Montrose Ave., Chicago, where Jesse Shannon's son Max was president (114). At this writing, the great-great-offspring of the Shannon Twin Spinner is the twenty-first-century War Eagle spinner bait, produced by Keith Brashers of Rogers, Arkansas, and still sold by a single distributor (115).

The Shannon Twin Spinner was weedless, It employed a single long-shank upturned hook with two resilient wire arms secured to the foremost portion of the shank at the eye. The hook lay behind and below the free ends of the arms, which were spaced apart on opposite sides of the hook and which extended upward and rearward to lie above the hook's pointed end. A swivel mounted on the free end of each arm had reflecting blades at the end. The vibrasonic blades that cause the radiation of sonic vibrations are placed to conceal the hook and were positioned in such a way that a strike at the reflective surface would result in a hooked fish.

Over the years, the old faithful enticer, oft celebrated for its effectiveness, has transitioned in and out of popularity in American bass angling. The Twin Spinner, used with or without an artificial or natural bait trailer, has a century of proven versatility. When it is used as a drop bait, the eye end of its shank travels downward first, resulting in a continuous flashing movement of the twin blades, and the upward-turned hook allows the lure to crawl over obstructions while slowly rolling across the bottom to fish deep structure. Jason Lucas, one-time editor of *Sports Afield* magazine, described his experiments with Shannon's spinner bait, a known tool for obstructed water, in the March 1968 edition: he said that it also paid him "in bass caught, to use it in perfectly open water" (114).

### The Creek Chub Bait Company's No. 100 Wiggler (1916)

In 1916, Creek Chub Bait Company (CCBC) of Garrett, Indiana, introduced the archetype combination floating/diving lure, the No. 100 Wiggler. When not reeled, the lure would float; when reeled, it would go underwater and travel with a wobbling motion. Many anglers would learn to appreciate this new genre of lures having the ability to function as a surface popper or floating jerkbait but also, when retrieved, as a shallow-running crankbait; thus the floating/diving lure quickly became a primary baitcasting tool.

H. S. DILLS,
FISH BAIT.
APPLICATION FILED DEC. 18, 1915.

**1,352,054.**                                    Patented Sept. 7, 1920.

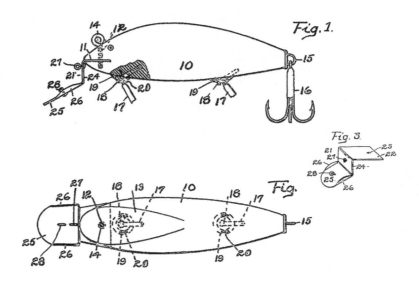

Creek Chubb patent drawing

The ability of the Wiggler to perform both surface and diving functions was possible because of the unique diving lip (mouthpiece) invented by Henry Dills. Apparently Dills conceived an idea for producing a wiggling-type bait as early as 1906, when he shared thoughts with George Schulthess and Carl Heinzerling (116). The story has it that the three men experimented and discussed fishing ideas while angling at Lake Wawasee in Indiana (116). They established the Creek Chub Bait Company as a corporation in 1918, two years after the initial production run of the new lure. The Henry Dills patent, applied for on December 18, 1915, was awarded on September 7, 1920, US Patent 1,352,054.

The lure came from the factory with the lip inserted into a slot at the nose of the lure and fastened in place by a vertical screw eye positioned at the top of the lure. The main line-tie protruded horizontally through the center portion of the lip, which formed the only attachment to the wood lure. In this position, the lure functioned as a deep-diver.

Creek Chub No. 100 Wiggler

According to the patent, fastening the line to the vertical screw eye at the top of the lure that held the lip in place, instead of at the main line-tie, allowed the lure to function as a near-surface diver. This feature may not have worked as originally conceived by Dills, because the 1922 CCBC catalog provided an illustration depicting the near-surface mode of operation which stated that the mouthpiece should actually be removed from the bait.

The patented diving lip, subsequently used on numerous other Creek Chubb lure models, deserves remembrance as one of the innovations that expanded the functionality of the baitcasting system by giving the sport the first floating/diving crankbait.

### Nick and Cosma Creme's Wiggle Worm (1949)

In the 1940s Nick Creme and his wife, Cosma, made their home in Akron, Ohio, a city of approximately 275,000 people, where the post–World War II economic boom had created jobs. Akron, the heart of America's rubber industry, employed more than eighty-five thousand rubber workers (117); Nick, smart and inquisitive, was one of them. He also loved to fish, and one day he became tired of digging for worms. The idea of making an artificial worm, at first a fleeting thought, eventually became an obsession. Nick had no background in chemistry, but because of his job, he knew people who did. Soon, through research and information provided by friends, he decided that rubber was unsuitable as worm material and that new plastics offered more potential. This insight led Nick to visit the Cleveland facility of DuPont, a company deeply involved in engineering polymers. There a lab technician generously gave him chemicals for experiments.

Nick and Cosma spent months experimenting with polymer, pigments, and oils in their home kitchen. Finally, having discovered a formula and process, they poured the newly engineered material into a mold that Nick had made from an actual night crawler. The result was a plastic worm that elongated, contracted, and jiggled like the real thing. The Creme Wiggle Worm, the archetype of soft plastic worm bait, became a reality in 1949. Nick and Cosma began selling by mail in packages of five. When almost ten thousand packs were sold at the Cleveland Sportsman's Show, their kitchen became too small. They moved the work into a small manufacturing plant, but the worm's deadly effect on bass continued to increase product demand.

In the late 1950s Creme became aware of the huge amounts of worm shipments to Texas. Although he did not realize it yet, his worm had appeared at the best possible moment in history, the peak time when dam and reservoir construction reached completion. In July 1964, when the Texas Water Commission published their comprehensive report, the state dams and reservoirs numbered well into the hundreds. The top twenty reservoirs according to storage capacity accounted for over one million acres of surface area; the largest, the Toledo Bend Dam and Reservoir, measured 186,500 acres (118). The reservoir water that covered previously wooded and thicketed areas created first-rate protection for bass. Traditional lures could not penetrate the obscured environment of trees, bushes, and other foliage.

It did not take long for a crafty angler to devise a technique for rigging the Wiggle Worm to fish the Texas reservoirs. Angling lore says that an unknown angler cut the brass pin out of a bell sinker, threaded the line through the hole, tied a hook to the end, ran it through the head of the worm, and buried the hook point into the worm's body—presto, the famous Texas Rigged Worm.

After the new rigging concept became general knowledge, Creme could not keep up with the demand. He eventually built a facility in Tyler, Texas, which remains there at this writing. Many top bass anglers agree that the artificial worm is as popular in the twenty-first century as it ever was and consider Creme's original straight-tail worm, made so realistic from the very beginning, as the best of the soft plastic baits.

### Lauri Rapala's Original Floating Wobbler (1936)

The Rapala Original Floating Wobbler was invented by a down-to-earth Finnish angler who made an observation of simple genius: "Big fish eat little fish, especially little fish that are wounded" (119). While rowing his boat on Finland's Lake Paijanne and studying fish, Lauri Rapala became aware that predator fish would shoot into a school of minnows and strike the one appearing to swim with a somewhat off-center wobble as if injured (120).

Rapala was a "kind, humble man" who "really understood fishing" (120); he could read the water, understood fish movement, and knew the effects of weather. Living through a very difficult period during a European economic depression fueled in part by the Great Depression in the United States, Rapala worked desperately to support his family. Out of necessity, he reaped as many pounds of fish as possible. He designed an artificial lure to catch more fish, earn money, and ditch the live minnows, which he harvested from a nearby forest lake. In 1936 he made his first successful lure from cork, "using a shoemaker's knife and some sandpaper" (120). To provide the necessary reflective outer coating, he used materials from discarded chocolate bar tinfoil and melted photographic negatives.

Original Floating Wobbler

(Courtesy of the History of Fishing
Museum, Branson, MO)

The other part of Rapala's realization about big fish eating little fish is "that which is irresistible to fish will always be irresistible to the fisherman." Extending through 140 countries, the Rapala empire has total global sales that put twenty million new Rapala lures into anglers' tackle boxes every year (119). In 2015 Rapala VMC Corporation, the global market leader in fishing lures, operated the largest distribution network in the industry, manufactured an array of popular lures in five countries, and employed some 3,200 people in thirty-nine countries with recorded net sales of $317 million. (121) With an exceptional record of global expansion, Rapala has helped millions of anglers catch fish. It all started with the Rapala Original Floating Wobbler, one of the most productive crankbait type lures ever produced.

# Chapter 10

# THE LAST KENTUCKY REEL MAKER

*1866 to 1948*

## George William Gayle

The story of Clarence Gayle, the last of the Kentucky artisans producing handmade reels for actual angling use, fittingly begins with his artisan father, George William Gayle, born June 3, 1834. George Gayle worked as an apprentice for a short period, concurrently with B. C. Milam, in the Frankfort watchmaking and reel-making business of J. F. and B. F. Meek. Evidently Gayle's association occurred around 1848, after Milam's release from the US Army but prior to his becoming a business partner with the Meeks. Although apprenticed to the Meeks for only a brief time, Gayle was intimately familiar with this group of artisans; according to the 1850 US census, Gayle resided in the B. F. Meek family home. Noted as a skilled artisan, Gayle subsequently worked for the Worsham P. Loomis jewelry business, located next door to the Meek and Milam shop. There Gayle made watches and managed the business until Loomis died in 1870, when the business closed (122).

## Clarence Gayle

George Gayle's son, Clarence Gayle, born November 15, 1866, inherited his father's artisanship. As a child, Clarence attended formal elementary school through the third grade (123); later, as a young teenager, he too worked with B. F. Meek and B. C. Milam. Through that association, a keen interest in reel making began to emerge.

When Clarence was about sixteen, he and his father formed the George William Gayle & Son company. There was some question as to whether George or Clarence actually made the first Gayle reel; however, Clarence answered the question in the article "Hand-Made Reels" that he wrote for the May 1905 issue of *The Sporting Goods Dealer*. Clarence stated, "When the writer was a mere boy he helped his father, George W. Gayle, make the first 'Gayle' reel. This was somewhere along in the early '80's" (71).

Gayle family literature indicates 1882 as the date of the first Gayle reel, a brass No. 3 size made for Lent Tanner, a relative (122). It is stamped "Geo. W. Gayle & Son" and inscribed with Tanner's initials and an 1884 date (122), but Gayle family tradition holds that the reel was date-stamped two years following its manufacture. The other brass reel in the family's possession is a small No. 1 size marked 1885, made for Tanner's sister, Sadie, the wife of Clarence's older brother Herbert (122).

Clarence Gayle (left) and B. F. Meek making reels in Frankfort
(Courtesy of the Gayle family)

# The New Gayle Reel (1897)

The Gayle partnership continued to produce the familiar type of Kentucky reel. However, sometime in 1895, about a year before his father George died on September 24, 1896, Clarence introduced a new style of handmade reel, which became known as the "top hat" because of its raised gearbox. Advertised in the official program of the Second Scientific Angling Tournament held by the Chicago Fly Casting Club on August 13–14, 1897, it was a No. 3 size reel and sold for fifteen dollars (100). Other than the gearbox, the reel appeared to offer features generally found standard on most reels made by Meek and Milam; for example, it had a quadruple multiplying design, was constructed of German silver with a tempered steel pinion and pivots, and had screw-off oil caps similar to those employed by later Meek reels.

An interesting side note: the 1897 tournament, one of the first to offer competition for baitcasting accuracy and distance, replaced the hard-to-see ½-ounce dipsey casting weight with a rubber frog previously used as a fishing lure (100). Anglers using the 1897 Gayle reel, often deployed lures such as that artificial frog in lieu of live bait to catch bass.

New style Gayle raised gearbox reel: Intrinsic model
sold by William Mills & Son N. Y.

In 1900 an updated Gayle reel was advertised in the official program of the Third Scientific Angling Tournament held on August 17 and 18. It was marketed as the "Special 'V. L. & A.' Pattern" (referring to Von Lengerke & Antoine tackle distributors). It was offered in sixty- and eighty-yard sizes, which sold for fifteen and sixteen dollars respectively. The reel sported unique features, the most important of which was a large barrel spool that eliminated the necessity of building up the spindle with old line in order to cast more easily. Additional features included "extra light gearings and light spools" (100). Those innovative premium features, which helped eliminate line overrun (backlash), had been generally unavailable to the average angler.

In addition to Von Lengerke & Antoine, another national tackle supplier, William Mills & Son, began marketing Gayle reels under the "Intrinsic" moniker. Although marketed nationally by two famous distributors, these reels remain exceedingly rare. About this time, mass-produced Kentucky reels and other more recent types were flooding the market, and Gayle had a rough go of it financially. In 1905 Gayle left behind his family and the city of Frankfort to take a position in Flint, Michigan, within the manufacturing tooling department of Buick Motors. In one of his letters back home to his wife, he stated that Buick wanted to adjust his pay and give him stock in the company instead. He said this was unacceptable, as he had two boys he was trying to get through college. He had been sending home five to twenty dollars each month to help support the family (123). Subsequently Gayle ended up working in a similar position with Harley Davidson in Aurora, Illinois (124).

## The Simplicity Reel

On November 11, 1918, the Frankfort *State Journal* published an article titled "Clarence Gayle Awarded Contract by Government." The article re-lated that Gayle, who had been in charge of Harley Davidson machinists in Aurora, Illinois, but was now back in Frankfort, had received a three-year government contract to produce cutting tools for production of steam boil-ers and ship plates for the navy. What a remarkable announcement, since that particular day was Armistice Day, the end of World War I. Although I do not want to rain on Clarence's parade, one might believe that at war's end, new military contracts would be a dubious endeavor. Regardless, the article also divulged that Gayle was producing thousands of cheap reels for distribution all across the country (125). This is worthy of note because the "cheap reels," better known as the Simplicity line of reels, are generally thought to have first been produced much later, in the 1920s.

Gayle's Simplicity reel, an extremely low-cost, stamped-out, single-action fly reel designed for anglers who could not afford a Kentucky reel, was marketed internationally. In the United States, it was sold for fifty cents by the F. W. Woolworth Company (126), a discounted merchandise, five-and-dime type store. Japanese manufacturers, interested in the Simplicity reel because of its high level of functionality and extremely low production cost, fabricated a copy. To be precise, they made an exact copy, with the makers' mark "Gayle Simplicity, Frankfort Kentucky USA" on one side and "Made in Japan" on the other. Understandably, this deeply disturbed and annoyed Gayle. It got worse. Gayle's Woolworth contract was not renewed, even though the reels had been successfully completed and delivered. It seems Woolworth began procuring the reels from Japan because their product was cheaper (126). Gayle, now the financial victim of a knockoff, continued to be abused. The Japanese imitations appeared for sale in Woolworth stores across the United States at the original retail price (126). The story of Gayle's Simplicity reel is easy to believe in modern times, when countries like China have pirated every product known to humankind.

## Gayle the Angler

Clarence Gayle is one of four Kentucky reel makers known to have participated in the sport of baitcasting; the others were George Snyder, J. F. Meek, and J. L. Sage. A passionate angler who fished Elkhorn Creek and the Kentucky and Dix Rivers (122), Gayle used the reels he had made for himself. Interestingly, numerous family photographs show him using a Simplicity No. 5, one of his mass-produced products. As an indication of how much he enjoyed angling, he produced a reel for his fiancée Emma Kavanaugh prior to their marriage on June 18, 1890. It was an undated No. 1 size Kentucky reel with red, hard rubber side plates (122).

During the 1930s Gayle produced and marketed a small line of artificial lures. An advertisement in the Frankfort *State Journal* on October 3, 1936, illustrates both a Simplicity reel and a wooden fishing lure. Regarding the lure, priced at twenty-five cents, the article states, "This cut shows our Kentucky Steel-Back 'Shorty' Bait... finished in five attractive color combinations. When fish are striking at all you can get them with a 'Shorty.'" Gayle named the lure after his grandson, Joe A. "Shorty" Gayle. The Shorty lure came in two variations. Both were surface/diving types, slightly longer than three inches, with metal diving lips stamped with Gayle's mark and two treble hooks. The version pictured in the above-mentioned advertisement had a lure nose cut at an angle, whereas the other version had a bulbous nose.

The Gayle product line also included the Steelback, a slim six-inch surface lure with a propeller fore and aft, each stamped with Gayle's mark, and three treble hooks. No doubt Gayle named that lure after the steelbacked minnow, commonly found in Kentucky water and a favorite live bait choice of early Kentucky anglers. Interestingly, according to Currey Gayle, Clarence's great-grandson, family tradition says that Clarence did not enjoy lure production because he could not resolve the issue of paint chipping and flaking off the lures he produced (123).

In addition, Gayle produced the "Draw 'Em All" lure, a simple undulated worm-style lure with two double hooks attached to the split ring on the rear and a brass box swivel on the front. The card affixed to the lure described it: "With all the advantages and none of the defects of natural shell, this bait is tough and strong and will stand the hardest use without chipping or breaking. When drawn through the water it has a decided wiggling motion that DRAWS the attention of fish. PEARLY rays radiating from all sides penetrate the water in every direction and are a further attraction to all fish."

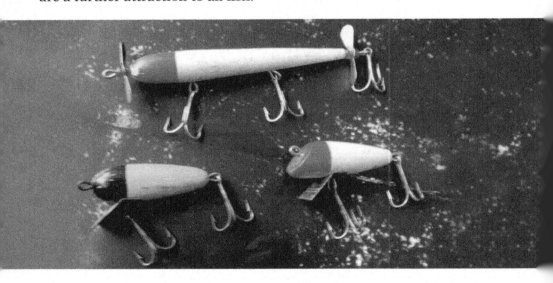

Clarence Gayle lures
(Courtesy of the Gayle family)

## Future Reel-Making Plans 1929–1937

In the fall of 1929, Robert Page Lincoln interviewed Clarence Gayle and discussed "the reel makers, the history of the reel and Gayle's plans for the future" (38). Noted in the interview was that Gayle had stopped producing handmade reels ten years previous. In addition, Lincoln asked Gayle if he "would again go into the manufacture of hand-made Kentucky reels to keep up the reputation of Frankfort" (38). Although Lincoln does not record Gayle's reply verbatim, he paraphrased it with "He said so," in essence saying there was a possibility Gayle would consider it (38). Furthermore, Gayle indicated that any additional income from producing more handmade reels was unimportant; his reason for possibly doing so would be "leaving behind me after I am gone something by which I will be remembered by the very best class of people on earth—the real sportsman angler" (38).

Eventually Gayle did resume production. A 1937 Geo. W. Gayle & Son catalog advertised some very fine reels: the traditional Kentucky reel in eight different sizes, priced at $100 for the small and medium-sized reels and $125 for the larger sizes. Additional features included jeweled bearings for $6 and pearl handles for $1.00 to $2.50 depending on the size. Using sterling silver in lieu of German silver cost an extra $15 to $50 depending on the size.

The catalog also displayed Gayle's newer Top Hat raised gearbox reel, made with either a balanced or twin-style handle and including a swinging thumb drag (a type used before the star drag became available) for medium to heavy fishing. Those reels sold for $100 to $200, depending on size. One fly-casting reel, the Gayle Aluminum Trout Reel, appeared in two sizes: a 2¼-inch diameter holding twenty-five yards of trout or bass line, priced at $30, and a four-inch diameter salmon reel at $75.

The same catalog contains an article titled "Concerning 'Gayle' Hand Made Fishing Reels, Made in Frankfort, Kentucky by George William Gayle & Son for 53 Years." The article confirmed the close relationships among the old community of artisans who produced the Kentucky reels. The article also highlighted the special relationship between George Gayle and his son Clarence. It stated of Clarence, "It has been to his privilege and to his immense mechanical profit to have been trained by his father, Geo. W. Gayle, and to have known intimately and to have had much valuable advice and passed many pleasant hours with Ben F. Meek, Ben C. Milam and John Milam, his son."

## Government Subcontract Work

Prior to and following the United States' entry into World War II, industrial production related to government requirements increased. Work from US government contracts awarded to major manufacturers soon flowed to subcontractors, and some found its way to Frankfort, Kentucky. Clarence Gayle—a highly competent manufacturing and tooling engineer, probably better described as combination mechanical engineer and master machinist of the highest order—was on the cutting edge of the tooling, equipment, and processes necessary for producing machined products. In addition, he was familiar with the stringent processes of government contract work. Consequently, Gayle played a key role as a subcontractor in America's war effort by producing key parts for weapons systems.

The United States entered the Second World War on December 7, 1941, when the Japanese attacked the US naval base at Pearl Harbor. On May 30, 1943, Clarence Gayle became engaged in the war effort when he was awarded a subcontract by the F. H. Lawson Company of Cincinnati, Ohio, to produce parts for floating bombs for the US military. Beyond his patriotic motives as an American, Gayle had a personal interest in helping the Allies win the war. His son, Lt. Col. Coburn Gayle, and three grandsons were engaged in the fight; additionally, the previous injustice he suffered at the hands of the Japanese over his loss of the Simplicity fishing reel contract still pained him (127). Consequently, Gayle put forth an effort that would soon draw acclaim from the highest levels.

When he was awarded a second subcontract—this time from Clinton Engineer Works, a contractor associated with the government's national laboratory at Oak Ridge, Tennessee—Gayle needed to prepare for a major task. His small shop, located behind his home at 514 Logan Street in Frankfort, required significant enlargement as well as a complement of machine tools, special tooling, and general plant equipment to perform the work he was about to undertake. There was also another resource, now in short supply, that required his attention: employees to do the work. He hired local construction workers to enlarge and revamp his shop into a small factory and began to fill the ranks of the required technical and support workers. Gayle enlisted local Kentucky farmers, homemakers, retirees, and a few high school students to obtain the necessary number of twenty-eight employees (127). Simultaneously, he worked to obtain the special tooling and general equipment he needed.

The job for Clinton Engineer Works would involve production of approximately thirty thousand parts with twenty different part numbers—no small effort. To complicate matters, the part drawings requiring his review and analysis were highly controlled by the government. Nonetheless, Gayle persisted in acquiring the proper tools to do the job at a time when generally available resources were already employed producing essential war supplies in other factories throughout the country.

A precision lathe was required, the type that B. C. and John Milam had used in their Frankfort shop many years before. Gayle had purchased that lathe along with the other contents of Milam's shop when John Milam died in 1928. However, he had later sold the lathe to one Edmund Rod-

man. Now in a crisis, Gayle contacted Rodman and arranged a two-year use agreement for work on the newest government contract (124).

Gayle, using the equipment he scraped together, successfully met his contractual requirements. Timely delivery of the products led to their incorporation into America's first atomic bomb, deployed to defeat the Japanese and win World War II. Because of the highly specialized and critical work Gayle performed, he was personally congratulated by General Henry H. "Hap" Arnold, commanding general of the US Army Air Forces and the only Air Force general to hold the five-star rank.

Ironically, cheated by the Japanese out of a nice income formerly realized by the annual sale of a hundred thousand Simplicity reels, Gayle became an essential component in ending one of history's bloodiest conflicts. After it was all over, while chatting with one of his grandsons wounded during the war, he said, "I guess I got even with the SOBs." The grandson was Joe A. Gayle, the namesake for the little "Shorty" fishing lure.

## The Sea Sleds

Clarence Gayle, known as "an ardent sportsman" (128), nurtured his affinity for the Kentucky waters. He loved to fish and make tackle, became an expert swimmer, and is known to have built canoes, skiffs, and house-boats. Sometime following 1913, when William Albert Hickman launched his invention, the Sea Sled, at the New York Motor Boat Show, Gayle developed a keen interest in the innovative watercraft's design. Gayle's inherent curiosity drove him to analyze the Sea Sled design and apply engineering principles to develop a larger model for use on Kentucky water.

Sea Sled Emma K 4

(Courtesy of the Gayle family)

Gayle built four Sea Sled–type watercraft and named each of them for his wife, Emma Kavanaugh Gayle: Emma K 1 through Emma K 4. The Sea Sled hull design somewhat resembled a catamaran. A tunnel in the shape of an inverted V beginning at the bow of the craft flattened out as it ran aft. When the boat moved quickly ahead, air trapped in the tunnel lifted the forward hull, allowing the craft to ride on a cushion of air. This design required less power, planed faster, carried a heavier load, and benefited from a shallower draft than other similarly sized watercraft.

In photographs of two of Gayle's Sea Sleds, the boats appear to be about twenty-five feet in length, with a flat deck enclosed by a short, horizontal three-plank fence. There is a flat-roofed rectangular cabin approximately ten feet in length with four-pane windows, apparently four on each side. One photo shows eight to ten people on board one of the boats and another six on shore in the process of boarding. Each of the Sea Sleds flew a nautical pennant flag made from the petticoats that Emma K. Gayle had worn under her 1890 wedding dress. A local Kentucky author and contemporary of Gayle noted that Gayle "has to his credit the manufacturer of some of the finest boats that Frankfort, as a river port, has ever seen" (128).

# The Gifts

It is unknown exactly how many handmade reels Gayle produced; however, his family believes it was approximately one hundred (123). He would continue to produce handmade reels in diminishing numbers following World War II. These final reels, similar to the earliest that he produced, were most likely made as gifts (45). The very last of these reels were marked "Hand Made," with Gayle's first initial and last name, "CGayle," engraved in script; Gayle reels were never serialized. A headline article in the Wednesday morning, September 8, 1948, edition of the Frankfort *State Journal* read, "Death Comes to Maker of Noted Reels, Clarence Gayle, 81, Expires Monday; Funeral today." The era of the Kentucky reel makers had passed away along with Gayle, the last and perhaps most talented Kentucky reel maker.

(Courtesy of the Gayle family)

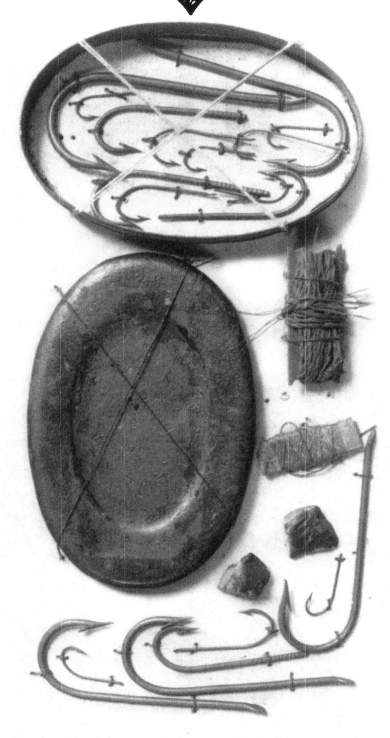

George Washington's Tackle

(Courtesy of the Library of Congress)

# Chapter 11

# TECHNOLOGY IMPROVES THE BAITCASTING SYSTEM

## *1880 to 1960*

## The Seamed Steel Rod

The progression of nineteenth- and twentieth-century technologies resulted in innovative uses for existing materials, supplies of new materials, and ingenious manufacturing processes for constructing the various components of the baitcasting system. These advancements proved essential for developing the sport because they offered superior functionality and durability along with reduced maintenance and cost.

The foundation of the system, the baitcasting rod, was the first to benefit. Initially rods were handmade by artisans from wood, bamboo, or a combination of the two materials. Bamboo offered unparalleled action, but was too expensive for the angler with a limited budget. A fully functional, value-priced alternative was necessary if baitcasting were to advance.

As Ozark Ripley later pointed out, the steel baitcasting rod filled that need and was a primary factor in the fast growth of the sport.

> Few appreciate what the coming of the steel rod did for bait casting. Probably it did more towards recruiting followers of the game than anything else. The cheap price of some steel rods made it convenient for people of the most modest means to own one that was really serviceable. In addition progressive bait casting ideas were incorporated in them, which even the best makers of high quality bamboo rods soon had to emulate. (107)

The steel rod praised by Ripley is a type that began with Everett Horton, a resident of Bristol, Connecticut. An innovative mechanic, Horton constructed a highly portable, durable fishing rod made from telescoping steel tubes. On March 8, 1887, he received US Patent 359,153 for the new rod. This invention resulted in the formation of the famous Horton Manufacturing Company, which eventually produced a complete line of steel fishing rods. By the early 1900s, the new telescoping rod became one of the most popular in America.

Horton's rod became an example for numerous manufacturers who built hollow-rolled steel rods of varying designs, actions, and lengths for all types of angling. However, no matter the action or shape, each of these rods shared several common characteristics. As part of the original design, hollow-rolled steel rods (both telescoping and individually sectioned) employed a lengthwise, unwelded running seam; consequently, the rod lacked the fine action of bamboo and the requisite strength. It was, however, serviceable and inexpensive.

## The Rapier Steel Rod

In 1928 Ripley wrote, "During the last few years an unexpected new type of steel rod appeared. Instead of being hollow and tubular in type as the recognized standard steel rod, it is made of solid steel just like a fencing foil" (107). The rod Ripley referred to, commonly called the rapier steel rod, has an excellent action and the strength to land the largest of freshwater fish. It also has a most interesting story that involves both a United States senator from Missouri and one of America's most renowned casting champions.

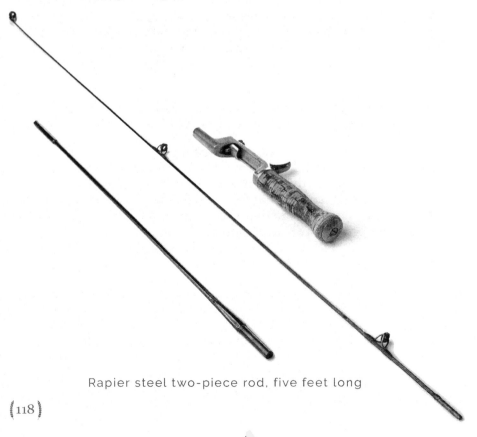

Rapier steel two-piece rod, five feet long

Harry B. Hawes (1869–1947)—US senator, congressional representative, Army officer, author, poet, and wildlife activist—was an avid angler who believed humans should practice chivalry not only in their relations with each other but also in their contact with nature and wild things. In his book *My Friend the Black Bass*, Hawes stated that he had a friend, a good boxer, fencer, and muskellunge angler, who had a short rod fashioned from a fencing foil; he could cast the heaviest lure for great distances with accuracy when using it. Later, having received a rapier rod from his friend, Hawes showed it to a number of his congressional associates, who all became interested in obtaining a similar one for their own use (129).

Hawes went on to say that he managed to recycle over four dozen discarded fencing foils, either by converting them to casting rods or by giving them to friends with instructions on how to produce their own rods. He also said that although manufacturers had adapted and improved the idea, he is certain his friend was the originator of the first solid steel rod (129).

The American Fork and Hoe Company (later True Temper) started marketing the rapier steel rod in 1925. The rod, famous for a limber action, is also incredibly strong and exceptionally durable. A recent examination of a fine example of a two-section rapier rod revealed that it has a surprisingly nice action and is still a first-rate rod for casting ½-ounce lures.

Fred Arbogast, a decorated tournament caster, national baitcasting champion, national grand champion fly caster and prolific tackle manufacturer, used a solid steel baitcasting rod. While angling with Arbogast on a canoe trip in Ontario, Robert Page Lincoln, another eminent angler, asked about his partner's rod. Arbogast related that he used a Toledo solid steel rod that was ground to his specifications; he then presented Lincoln with one (102). In 1952 Lincoln related that he used Arbogast's generous gift over some twenty years' time and caught the largest muskellunge of his life (forty-six pounds) with it. Although he eventually put the rod aside (save for muskie fishing), undoubtedly for rods made of newer, more technologically advanced materials, Lincoln stated that "in its day, as a general rod, it had points of value not to be slighted. I do know that Fred Arbogast, who was a discriminating caster, regarded the Toledo steel rod very highly" (102).

## Detachable Rod Handle with Offset Reel Seat

Another enhancement that appeared alongside the solid steel rod was the one-piece detachable rod handle featuring a reel seat offset laterally from the axis of the rod, patented by W. B. Zass (US Patent 1,534,674) on April 21, 1925. The new handle served three purposes: the rear of the handle formed the handgrip; the middle section provided a downward-extending reel seat; and the forward section supplied the socket to hold the rod in place.

In addition, the lowered reel seat had the effect of aligning the reel spool with the rod's axis, in contrast to the old method that mounted the reel on top of the rod, above the axis. This new configuration gave the thumb of the angler's casting hand comfortable access to the revolving line spool and provided a trigger-style finger grip for the index finger, thereby offering better control.

Later, the Shakespeare Company offered an enhanced version of the one-piece handle and was awarded a patent on October 21, 1941 (US Patent 2,260,204). The company's research and development showed that employing a handgrip in line with the axis of the rod, as Zass did, impeded casting accuracy and promoted wrist strain. The reason is that when an angler executes a cast, the rod handle tends to align itself with the arm of the caster, which is actually at an angle from the line of aim between the caster's eye and the target spot. Therefore, unless the wrist is cocked toward the right (in the case of a right-handed angler), the cast has a tendency to go to the left of the intended target. Furthermore, cocking the wrist to one side eventually results in fatigue. Shakespeare's invention solved the problem by changing the angle of the grip relative to the socket holding the rod in place.

## One-Piece Seamless Hollow-Steel Rod

In his 1947 book *With Fly, Plug, and Bait*, Ray Bergman said that the best general-purpose baitcasting rod was "a 5½ foot lightweight new type steel rod" (130). This latest version of the steel rod had a tubular, one-piece, seamless construction made possible by twentieth-century technology. It supplanted the rapier steel rods used by Arbogast, which had previously replaced the earlier Bristol-style seamed rods. Bergman recommended the seamless steel rod because of the fine bamboo-like action it possessed.

Often made by True Temper or Heddon, the seamless tubular steel rods were the finest available and took the sport by storm. Robert Page Lincoln stated that this type of rod "was revolutionary in conception and its action, strength and one piece (construction).... No item of tackle so captivated the universal fancy of the bait caster" (102). He estimated that eighteen of twenty baitcasters used the seamless steel rod, the remaining two preferring bamboo. These rods remained popular until the early 1950s, when newer materials generally became available to the tackle industry.

# Fiberglass Is Invented

Scientific discovery made evolution of the baitcasting rod possible by unlocking the secrets for creating new and unique materials. Until the early twentieth century, natural resins from plants and animals were the only glues and binders to be had for cementing products together; but when scientists developed plastics, rod composition began to progress. Plastic by itself lacked the strength and rigidity for fishing rods, so another material needed to be added.

During the mid-1930s, one such material surfaced through the research and development efforts of a new company created by a partnership between two large glasswork manufacturers, Corning Glass and Owens-Illinois. The Owens-Corning Fiberglas [*sic*] Corp. produced a material originally known as glass wool but later known as fiberglass (131). When glass fiber is combined with plastic, it creates a composite, fiber-reinforced polymer—a perfect material for fishing rods. Fiberglass-reinforced plastic boat hulls, first produced in 1944, became one of the largest applications for fiberglass reinforcements (131). Fiberglass baitcasting rods would soon follow.

# Fiberglass Rods and Dr. Howald's Process

The research and development conducted to support America's World War II effort brought about the development of many new products, and the sport of baitcasting was a beneficiary. Because of military research in 1946, Dr. Arthur Howald, an avid angler and coincidentally a technical director at the Libby-Owens-Ford Glass Co., patented a process for making tubular fiberglass. After Howald repaired his broken fly rod using a section of fiberglass tubing, he quickly realized that the tube material might be a viable alternative to bamboo. Howald conducted experiments and documented a fabrication process that he eventually provided to the Shakespeare Company. Shakespeare refined the process for mass production and began manufacturing fiberglass rods (132).

Other manufacturers also started producing fiberglass rods in two basic design types: hollow and solid. Each type had advantages. Hollow rods were lighter, but therefore broke more easily; solid rods were stronger, but heavier and more expensive (132).

Shakespeare, a highly inventive company, found a way to balance the positive characteristics of both types of rods by combining a hollow rod butt with a solid tip. They were able to produce this lightweight, yet strong product that sold at a highly competitive price by using two discrete manufacturing operations. The first operation produced a hollow rod core by wrapping fiberglass cloth around a tapered shaft; the core became the butt end of the rod. Next, fiberglass fibers were laid lengthwise along the core and extended beyond the narrow end some distance to form the solid, strong tip. This innovative two-step process became known as the Howald process (132).

## The Wonder Rod and the Ugly Stik

The first fiberglass rods introduced by Shakespeare during their fiftieth anniversary year in 1947 were white in color and bore the trade name Wonder Rod (133). These early rods became the model for the now famous Shakespeare Ugly Stik, first produced in 1976 (132). The Ugly Stik is significantly stronger than the early rods because the inner layer of material is graphite instead of fiberglass. It employs pigmented fibers to improve the cosmetic appearance, but retains clear tip fibers for recognition and marketing purposes.

By the twenty-first century, graphite replaced fiberglass for many angling applications; however, the fiberglass rods are not outdated. Material and manufacturing process improvements have kept fiberglass highly competitive, especially when the angler desires both a softer action and toughness for throwing modern crankbaits.

From Silk to Nylon

# New Metals and Alloys

Rods were not the only component of the baitcasting system to benefit from materials engineering. New metals and new alloys enhanced reels by increasing durability and maintainability and reducing weight.

The Kentucky reel had always been made of brass, German silver, or (rarely) sterling silver; most examples are German silver. This material, named for its enhanced development by nineteenth-century German metalworkers and for its silvery appearance, actually contains no silver. It is an alloy of copper, nickel, and zinc that has existed for over two thousand years. Also known as nickel silver, this extremely hard and abrasion-resistant material (134) proved to be the perfect metal for Kentucky artisans to work their magic. German silver is capable of being shaped, cast, rolled, stamped, forged, drawn, extruded, and machined. It is also nonmagnetic, and when exposed to oxygen for long periods, it develops a protective brownish-green patina (134) that most ardent collectors never, ever polish off. The material withstood the test of time. But in August 1913, time finally caught up with German silver when Harry Brearley invented stainless steel, a new alloy containing chromium, carbon, and steel (135).

About the same time, another material, aluminum, became generally available. The most abundant metal on earth and one of the most recently discovered, aluminum is always found naturally combined with other elements. There was no known economical way to separate and extract aluminum from the other elements until 1886, when a new smelting process was discovered (136). By the turn of the twentieth century, aluminum began to be used in various ways. Clarence Gayle, the last of the Kentucky reel makers, used it to produce reels.

## German Silver to Stainless Steel (1947)

Aluminum and stainless steel quickly became part of everyday life. By the end of World War II, both metals attained widespread use due to their low production cost. Stainless steel and aluminum replaced German silver and various other metals in many products, including fishing tackle.

This may be easily observed by examining a common casting reel, the Shakespeare Marhoff model. Before 1947, the Marhoff was made in part of nickel silver; from 1947 forward, stainless steel. (Other models may also suffice as an example, but only high-end reels were initially made of German silver; most value-priced reels were made of chrome-plated brass, which is easily observed as the plating wears off.)

Shakespeare stamped date codes on their reels. The table below can be used to determine a date in close proximity to the actual manufacturing date of a specific reel. A Marhoff reel produced in 1946 is stamped with a date code of "GE" on the side plate, which is also inscribed "Nickel Silver." The 1947 version has a date code of "GD" on the side plate along with the inscription "Stainless Steel." To avoid confusion with numerals, Shakespeare did not include the letters "O" and "I" in the date code mix.

| A | B | C | D | E | F | G | H | J | K |
|---|---|---|---|---|---|---|---|---|---|
| 0 | 9 | 8 | 7 | 6 | 5 | 4 | 3 | 2 | 1 |
| L | M | N | P | Q | R | S | T | U | V |

Shakespeare date codes use two letters for the last two numerals of the year. The code marked on the reel may include letters from the first row above, the third row, or from a combination of both the first and third rows. For example, GD, GP, SP, and SD all mean 1947.

# Fishing Line

The last component of the baitcasting system due for a major enhancement was fishing line, a seemingly simple and uncomplicated component. From the early days of baitcasting, fishing line was produced from one of three natural products: cotton, linen (from the flax plant), or silk (produced by silkworms). Made much like rope, fishing line was either twisted ("laid") or braided together.

The process for making laid line consists of three steps. First, individual threads/fibers are twisted in the same direction to produce yarn. Next, the yarns are twisted together in the opposite direction to produce strands. Finally, the strands are twisted together again, in the first direction, to produce the line. Twisted line must be fused together at each end to prevent unraveling, and it kinks easily; therefore, it is incompatible with baitcasting reels. As a result, it was often tied to the end of a cane pole for still-fishing. Common twine or string is an example of laid line.

Braided line, formed by braiding individual threads together into strands and strands into line, is significantly stronger and more durable than twisted line. Pulling on a braided line forces the braiding to lock the threads into place; it is much the same principle as a finger trap toy. Braided line also stretches less than twisted line and has a more rounded shape.

## Silk

Until just prior to World War II, the preferred line choice of many sporting baitcasters was closely braided raw silk line of the smallest diameter, a size that could sustain lifting a ten-pound weight. In the measurement system of the period it was identified as an H size line, H being the smallest diameter and A the largest. One nagging issue with silk line is that if left wet after fishing, it will deteriorate. Consequently, line dryers, often in the form of collapsible wire wheels with hand cranks, became common tackle box accessories.

## Nylon (1938)

In 1938, fishing line started to change. Nylon, a synthetic product produced from coal, petroleum, air, and water, became one of the noteworthy inventions of the twentieth century. It was developed by Wallace Hume Carothers and patented on September 20, 1938, by E. I. du Pont de Nemours and Company of Wilmington, Delaware, better known as DuPont. The next year DuPont began marketing nylon monofilament fishing line, the first synthetic fiber made from a single extruded fiber of polyamide material. The product showed great promise due to its inherent ability to maintain strong knot strength and yet remain almost invisible in the water. However, this primitive monofilament proved sinewy and difficult to cast (137); as a result, silk line persisted.

## Dacron Braided Line (1952) and Stren Monofilament Line (1958)

Before anyone could resolve the technical issues associated with the new monofilament fishing line, the United States entered World War II. Virtually all types of nylon materials went to support the production of war articles such as parachutes and B-29 bomber tires (138). During the war, however, DuPont resumed earlier research with another synthetic fiber and in 1945 purchased the US patent rights for further development of this material: polyester. In 1950 DuPont produced a polyester fiber using a modified nylon technology; by 1952, braided polyester fibers with better consistency and durability than silk became a reality (139). Sold under the trade name Dacron, this was the first functional modern fishing line. Dacron line remained extremely popular until the 1970s (137) and remains in use for special angling applications in the twenty-first century.

Continued development by DuPont resulted in the reintroduction of monofilament line in 1958 under the trade name Stren (140). Since that day, monofilament line has become the preeminent choice of sport anglers worldwide.

Louis Rhead woodcut

# Chapter 12
# THE BATTLE AGAINST BACKLASH

*Circa 1900 to Present*

## The Backlash

When a lure is cast, the baitcasting rod's action propels it toward the target by initially overcoming the resistance of the inert reel spool. Once in flight, the speeding lure, pulling line from the spool, eventually slows down and loses trajectory, and the force drawing line from the spool decreases along with the lure's velocity. At the same time, the rotating reel spool, powered by centrifugal force, is moving faster than the lure, so it must be slowed and brought into alignment with the force pulling the line; if not, it will continue spinning, releasing loose line loops that wrap around each other to form a backlash. This often results in a tangled and knotted mess of jumbled-up fishing line that requires great patience and significant time to untangle prior to making another cast.

Many of today's anglers began casting artificial lures using modern reels that employ various internal and external controls to make casting easier. The modern reel significantly improved the process of regulating how the line feeds off the reel spool during a cast and thus greatly reduced the cause of backlash. If you have ever used a baitcasting reel that lacked features for controlling spool speed or adjusting casting tension for varying lure weights, you understand that it can be a humbling experience.

## The Baitcasting Reel Described

The baitcasting method of angling has employed a fishing reel generally defined along the lines of George Snyder's 1815 archetype and the Kentucky reels that followed it. Since then the reel, still discernible as a Kentucky lineage creation, has evolved, and many new features have considerably improved its functionality. Consequently, the description of the reel offered here takes into account features not prevalent on numerous reels produced prior to the 1950s.

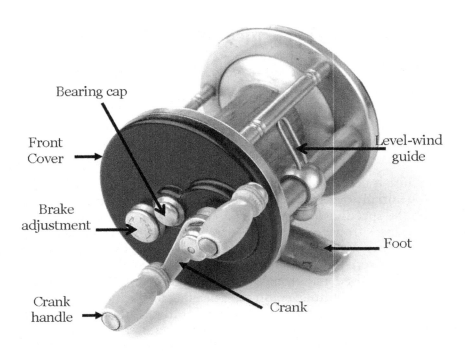

Bearing cap

Front
Cover

Brake
adjustment

Crank
handle

Level-wind
guide

Foot

Crank

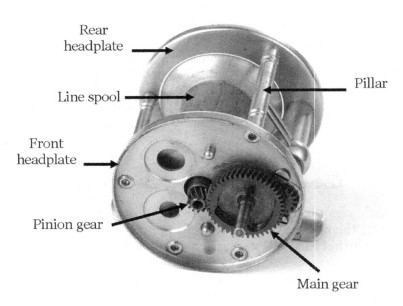

Rear
headplate

Line spool

Front
headplate

Pinion gear

Pillar

Main gear

J. A. Coxe 25-3 reel used by John F. Babler Sr. from 1946 to 2000

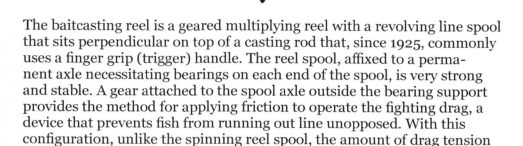

The baitcasting reel is a geared multiplying reel with a revolving line spool that sits perpendicular on top of a casting rod that, since 1925, commonly uses a finger grip (trigger) handle. The reel spool, affixed to a permanent axle necessitating bearings on each end of the spool, is very strong and stable. A gear attached to the spool axle outside the bearing support provides the method for applying friction to operate the fighting drag, a device that prevents fish from running out line unopposed. With this configuration, unlike the spinning reel spool, the amount of drag tension set by the angler does not affect the line spool's rotational stability.

One turn of the reel's crank handle equals multiple turns of the reel spool. Originally, the gear ratio (the number of times the reel spool turns for each turn of the crank handle) was approximately four to one. For this reason, anglers initially called the reel the "quadruple multiplier." Modern versions of these reels often use higher gear ratios, such as five, six, or even seven to one, in order to better support certain angling techniques requiring faster lure retrieval. Additionally, modern reels employ a free-spool mechanism, which disengages the line spool from the gear train to facilitate uninhibited spool rotation during the cast, thus allowing the lure to be cast greater distances.

The majority of baitcasting reels produced since the 1920s have also included a level-winding mechanism to respool line evenly when the lure is retrieved, as well as some form of reel brake (often referred to as an anti-backlash device) to retard spool speed automatically during the cast. These two features are the topic of focus in this chapter because they promoted the sport by helping to reduce backlash; however, most early authors of angling literature believed that the anti-backlash device was chiefly responsible. Hand-guiding fishing line to respool the reel, even though it adds another step to the casting process, is a generally a more agreeable task than untangling a backlash. Consequently, the blameworthy backlash will receive the attention it deserves up to and including the modern solutions, which in some cases still may not completely eliminate the problem.

Steve Vernon, in his 1985 book *Antique Fishing Reels*, maintains that improvements to the baitcasting reel were often made possible by previous developments in design or materials engineering (141). This is a point worth remembering, especially as it applies to features designed to eliminate backlash.

# Two Types of Early Reel Brakes

Two of the earliest reels with anti-backlash controls generally available to the angler were the South Bend Anti-Backlash and the Redifor (later Pflueger-Redifor) Self- Thumbing reel. These reels used different approaches to accomplish the required spool control.

The South Bend 1131-A reel appeared in 1907. It was stamped with two patent dates ("SEP 5, 05" and "FEB 5, 07") related to its line-activated automatic anti-backlash feature. This feature used a heavy wire bail, pivoted on each side and extending across the line at the reel front, to reduce spool speed at the end of the cast. Line tension kept the wire bail in the up (off) position until spool speed decreased. At that point line tension slackened, dropping the bail to engage the friction brake shoe.

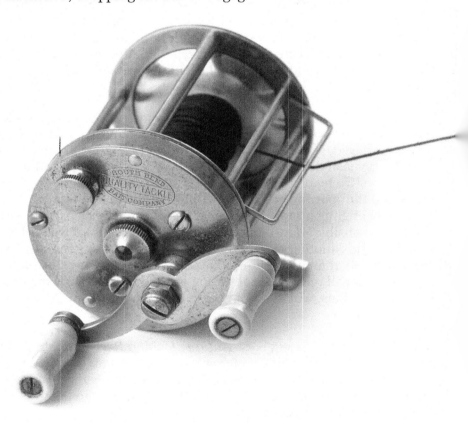

South Bend 1131-A friction brake

The Redifor Self-Thumbing reel used two centrifugally actuated brake shoes, located at the edge of the rear spool flange, that rotated outward against a machined recess in the rear head plate. The Redifor retarded spool speed at the beginning of the cast by forcing the brake shoes to the outside perimeter, increasing friction and keeping the spool from spinning too fast. As spool speed and resulting centrifugal force decreased, the two brake shoes pivoted away from the friction engagement position.

Redifor centrifugal brake

Thomas Hubert Hutton, author of the angling portion of *The Complete Angler and Huntsman*, tried to put the anti-backlash feature into perspective. He said, "The South Bend Anti-Back-Lash Reel . . . obviates entirely the necessity of thumbing the spool in casting. . . . It means that any man, woman or child who can hold a fishing rod may enjoy all the pleasures experienced by the seasoned angler, the very moment this reel is made part of the equipment" (142). Hutton's assessment is probably a little over the top, but it shows the importance of the early anti-backlash features.

## Level Wind Mechanism

It is interesting to note that neither the 1907 South Bend nor the 1908 Redifor anti-backlash control reel was equipped with a level wind mechanism, even though that feature was previously available on certain other reels. Before the level wind was invented, the angler used the index finger and thumb of the left hand to guide the retrieved line evenly onto the spool—not an easy task. Although not the root cause of backlash, a roughly wound line can certainly be a contributing factor. A lumpy, uneven, and possibly tangled line spool is not helpful to proper casting because it adversely affects the way line feeds off the spool through the rod guides.

The need for a form of mechanical line guiding goes back over 150 years. Various inventors worked on developing level wind mechanisms during the latter half of the nineteenth century. According to Vernon, Mark S. Palmer designed and patented a level wind as early as 1860 that remained "the design of choice" well into the twentieth century (141). However, the feature was not generally available until 1902, when Shakespeare's catalog advertised a level wind reel, the Shakespeare Model B. The advertisement stated its benefits.

> This beautiful reel has the level winding feature, which automatically spreads the line evenly on the spool. It is especially designed for accurate and long-distance bait casting. . . . Thousands of these level winding reels are in use, and not one has failed to give unbounded satisfaction.

The Shakespeare Model B reel used helical grooves cut into double shafts to operate the mechanism, a peculiar design that did not last. However, the company quickly marketed other designs for which they became famous. The level wind was a grand feature for the novice caster who succumbed to backlashes caused by lumpy, unevenly wound line spools.

Shakespeare Model B reel

## High-End Features in Value-Priced Product Lines

Prior to 1920, reels on the high end of the product spectrum included numerous mechanical innovations. These reels combined the level wind with anti-backlash control and a free spool; they appeared to tackle all the problems except that of cost. A 1920 product review of two premium reels, written by O. W. Smith, indicated a high level of satisfaction with the new reel features. Smith maintained that the Redifor Beetzsel and Pflueger Supreme reels both featured level wind mechanisms designed for friction-free casting, free-spool clutches, and self-thumbers (anti-backlash reel brakes) to alleviate backlash. Regarding the Pflueger, Smith indicated that if the angler does "not care to use the self-thumbing device simply set the arrow on the milled button at 'off' and the reel is a regular winch to be thumbed by the operator" (101). Smith put the price of the Pflueger at twenty dollars.

To help grow the sport's popularity, level wind and anti-backlash controls would need to be included as standard features in a value-priced line of casting reels for new recruits and less ardent anglers. This would be the true test for manufacturers. By 1930, a top-of-the-line reel cost twenty-five dollars; a fully serviceable, value-priced reel with level wind and anti-backlash features cost about five dollars.The reel manufacturers had succeeded in innovating and simplifying the casting process by providing serviceable, affordable tackle.

Redifor Beetzsel (left) and Pflueger Supreme (right)

## Spinning

The improvements made to the baitcasting reel, especially in regard to anti-backlash control and level wind features, proved sufficient until the spinning method gained momentum in the United States following World War II. The spinning method uses a multiplying reel that sits underneath the rod with the line guides facing down. It employs a stationary (non-rotating) line spool with the axis pointed in the direction of the rod. During the cast, line comes off the spool in coils, much like a spool of thread. The line is recovered (wound back) onto the spool by means of a revolving bail (arched metal arm) that disengages during the cast to allow the line to spiral freely off the spool.

Thommen Record spinning reel

Other than when casting and retrieving, the line spool necessarily rotates on the shaft that runs through it in order for the fighting drag device to operate. Unlike casting reels, the line spool shaft has bearing supports only on the gearbox side of the shaft; therefore, the spool has a tendency to wobble. The fighting drag, mounted on the front of the shaft, applies pressure to the front end of the spool and pushes it rearward against the reel to produce friction and stabilize wobble. The more the angler increases the pressure (by tightening the fighting drag against the spool), the more stable the spool becomes. When using lighter line, lower drag settings may be insufficient to stabilize the spool. Backlashes do not occur with a fixed spool reel; however, these reels are prone to line twist.

When compared to the conventional baitcasting reel, spinning had considerable appeal for the modern angler. It offered the ability to cast great distances while using light ¼-ounce and lighter lures. Almost immediately following the introduction of spinning, the minimally effective backlash controls on the baitcasting reel seemed old school and incapable of satisfying angler needs.

# The Spincasting Reel

Putting more distance between the multiplying reel and the modern angler was the introduction of the spincasting reel. This multiplying reel with a stationary line spool was ideal for beginning anglers because of its simple operation. The first two versions, invented and created independently and released to the public in 1949, made a big splash in the angling world: the Denison Johnson Model 20 Sidewinder and the Zero Hour Bomb Company (Zebco) Standard reel. Both the Johnson reel, invented by Lloyd Johnson and Warren Denison, and the Zebco reel, invented by Jasper R. Dell Hull, were under continuous product improvement. By 1955 both companies had advanced their now-famous designs, and the Johnson Century 100 and Zebco 33 were realities.

The primary objective of the spincasting reel was to eliminate the baitcasting reel's backlash, but retain its one-handed operation by eliminating the bail used on traditional spinning reels. This was accomplished by using a push-button line release to cast, and line pickup pins with a metal cone to rewind line. A secondary objective of the spincasting reel was to reduce the line twist sometimes encountered with other spinning reel designs. Similar to a spinning reel, line is thrown from a fixed spool; consequently, lightweight lures and baits can be deployed.

# A New Ambassadeur Arrives in America

In 1954, a novice angler using a spincasting reel could learn to cast in just a few minutes' time. As a result, baitcasting was losing the battle to attract new adherents to the sport. The reliable tried-and-true multiplying reel lagged well behind the ease of use and light tackle capability of either the spinning or the spincasting reel. Even highly proficient baitcasting experts saw merit in the new equipment, and many now included the new method as part of their repertoire.

At the 1954 New York World's Fair, the baitcasting reel received a new lease on life. It came in the form of the Ambassadeur 5000 reel produced by the ABU Corporation of Svangsta, Sweden (143). The Ambassadeur (spelled the French way because the language of international diplomats was French) had a plethora of features unavailable on American reels. These included a push-button, lightweight free-spool design to disengage the gear train; a star-shaped fighting drag to regulate tension on the outgoing line; an anti-reverse line spool; and for the caster still not proficient in thumbing a spool, a centrifugal brake mounted around the axis of the

reel spool in combination with a mechanical brake located on the end
of the spool shaft.

Backlash remained a significant issue with American baitcasting reels
of the early 1950s. It is true that manufacturers made improvements
following the introduction of the South Bend Anti-Backlash and the
Redifor Self-Thumbing reels some forty years previous; but often as not,
the improvements lacked substantial functionality. The Ambassadeur
5000 promised a rainbow at the end of the storm instigated by the rising
popularity of the spinning and spincasting reels. Of major import was
that the ABU Corporation's new reel included provisions for eliminating
backlash by employing a new combination centrifugal/mechanical brake.
Considering that the early Redifor Self-Thumbing reel had a centrifugal-
ly-actuated, friction-type brake, Vernon's opinion that improvement to
reels are often made possible by previous design seems to hold true.
The adage "What goes around comes around" appears applicable.

The Swedish reel offered great promise, as these words from a 1957
advertisement attest: "First bait-casting reel with free-running spool
combined with level-wind and centrifugal brake for backlash proof action.
. . . Anti-backlash centrifugal brake of famous Urfabriken construction.
Mechanical brake built into left spool cap with graduated scale to adjust
reel for different lures." Additionally, the owner information manual for
the new reel, under a major heading titled "The Importance of Balanced
Tackle," included exciting information about the reel's ability to handle
lightweight spinning tackle. It maintained that the reel could cast lures
weighing less than ¼ ounce at routine fishing distances if mounted on
a light-action six-foot rod using ten-pound braided line. More exciting,
if five-pound braided line or four-pound monofilament was used in
conjunction with a 6½-foot rod, 1/8-ounce spinning lures would cast well
because of the reel's extremely lightweight spool and smooth bearings.

The Ambassadeur reel proved to be the perfect product for the American
sport of baitcasting. In 1967, the year the Bass Anglers Sportsman's
Society (BASS) was formed, 27,072,000 fishing licenses were issued in
the United States (144). That same year, ABU produced 490,000
Ambassadeur 5000 reels. That is a ratio of one Ambassadeur reel for
every fifty-five fishing licenses. The total production of the Ambassadeur,
estimated at four million reels, marks the longest production run in the
history of multiplying reels (145). Interestingly, the Ambassadeur 5000
was the first baitcasting reel to function properly with monofilament line
(145). Imagine: a reel (actually designed in the mid-1940s) adept at using
four-pound mono and still capable of loading up with heavy braided line
and casting a two-ounce lure!

# Twenty-First Century Reel Brakes

Beyond the success of the Ambassadeur, many versions of twenty-first century multiplying reels continue to employ various types of brakes to mitigate backlash. The word "mitigate" rather than "eliminate" is used because some anglers, while using the most modern of reels, continue to experience line overrun, often caused by improper brake adjustment or inattention to casting technique. At this writing (2016), high-quality multiplying reels, available at various price levels, generally offer three types of brakes to control backlash: centrifugal brakes, magnetic brakes, and combination brakes.

### *Centrifugal Brakes*

Centrifugal brakes, commonly found on Shimano, Abu Garcia, and other reels, are friction-based and work best at the start of a cast to reduce backlash problems. Small, sliding brake blocks or pins, mounted around the axis point of the reel spool and forced to the outside perimeter by centrifugal force during the cast, rub against a brake ring, keeping the spool from spinning too fast. As the spool slows, centrifugal force is reduced and the pins slide inward and away from the brake ring. This allows the spool to keep spinning at the speed of the line pulled by the lure.

It became common for centrifugal brakes to utilize a six-pin system. Resistance control adjustments are made by first removing the side plate of the reel, a process that varies depending on the manufacturer. The six pins located inside the reel are always configured in a circular fashion around the axis point. Adjustments are made symmetrically, either by selecting two pins at a time that are located directly across from each other or by selecting every other pin. An adjustment never includes only one pin or five pins because that would prevent the brake from functioning properly. Pushing the pins outward engages the brake; to turn the brake off, pins are pushed back in until they click.

### *Magnetic Brakes*

Employed on reels made by Daiwa, Lew's, Abu Garcia, and other makers, magnetic brakes use magnetic force to keep the spool's speed in check. They often (but not always) operate throughout the cast, from beginning to end, even when little centrifugal force is operating. These brake designs use varying configurations of magnets and steel rings or disks to decrease the spool revolution rate. The amount of resistance depends on the distance between the magnets, which can be adjusted using a control on the outside of the reel. The type of control varies by manufacturer; most use a dial on the opposite side of the reel from the handle, with adjustments labeled from 0 to 10 or minimum to maximum.

*Combination Brakes*

Combination centrifugal/magnetic brakes, also known as dual systems, are popular as well. They appear on brands such as Pflueger, Bass Pro Shop, Abu Garcia, and other makes. Brake adjustments are made as described above, but resistance is generally set at lower levels.

## The Backlash-Free Reel

Interestingly, at this writing, one reel manufacturer is advertising two different models of what it calls a backlash-free reel. The lower-priced model is close to $300 and the higher just under $500. Videos presenting the reel in action are impressive, as they show the casting hand thumb totally off the line spool during the backlash-free casts. The manufacturer claims that unlike reels in which the pinion gear rides the spool shaft, this new system "floats the spool independently" on precision ball bearings. Because the pinion rides on its own separate shaft, the spool spins freely, unhampered by gear train friction when casting (146). Additionally, the manufacturer alleges that the redesigned level wind guide allows line to flow out freely through a wide top, thus eliminating friction when casting, and retrieves it through a narrow bottom for respooling (146).

In fact, the friction-free line guide was an innovative concept that reel manufacturers implemented long ago. Recall for a moment those high-end, pre-1920 reels that included numerous mechanical innovations. On both the Redifor and the Pflueger Supreme, the line was free of the guide during the cast but reengaged at the start of the retrieve. The tangible benefit advertised by the manufacturer of the twenty-first-century reel—reduction or elimination of outgoing line friction during the cast—has been available on the multiplying reel for about one hundred years.

Rose Cook (wife of Dixie Carroll)
(From Fishing, Tackle and Kits by Dixie Carroll)

# Chapter 13
# ANGLING BOATS AND MOTORS

*1881 to 2016*

## Meeting the Demands of Anglers

Baitcasting is a widely diversified sport supported by watercraft that must meet the needs of many and varying individuals. The variety of waterborne craft should leave few anglers dry-docked for a lack of choice.

A good freshwater fishing boat has always been one that meets the demands of the individual angler. When choosing a boat in the twenty-first century, anglers often consider particulars such as type of water fished, the species sought, and the method of angling employed. In the case of baitcasting, the method frequently becomes a discriminating factor because casting an artificial lure all day requires a safe, stable, and comfortable platform. Modern anglers are fortunate; the variety of choices offered by boat manufacturers to meet individual preferences does not disappoint many.

One hundred plus years ago, early twentieth-century anglers faced radically different choices when considering watercraft, and their preferences in boats were often associated with the way in which they traveled to the fishing locale. American lakes and streams that provided the best angling were difficult to reach in 1900. Railroads and steamboats compensated for the lack of automobiles; but after disembarking at the final rail terminal or boat dock, the angler may have had to travel many more miles to reach the camp destination. Complicating matters: once the angler arrived, fishing boats or any type of watercraft might be scarce or nonexistent. The inspired solution was for the angler to take a boat along—obviously a complicated task.

# The ACME Folding Boat

The Acme Folding Boat Company of Miamisburg, Ohio, had a vision of enabling North American anglers to reach obscure locales with a portable boat. Consequently, its designers devised a folding canvas rowboat that was flat-bottomed, ridged, and employed bituminous waterproofing. The canvas was "oiled and painted, thoroughly saturating it, so that it repels water like rubber," thereby protecting it from "mildewing and cracking" and "changes in temperature." The structure, "produced from high carbon, tempered spring steel," was galvanized and rustproof (147).

Acme folding boat

(Courtesy of the Miamisburg Historical Society, Ohio)

The folding boat, manufactured for more than fifty years, came in various sizes. In 1911, they ranged from nine feet to twenty feet long. The nine-foot model sold for twenty-five dollars, and the twenty-foot model was sixty-five dollars.

The nine-foot size had a thirty-two-inch beam and a depth of ten inches; it was rated to carry 350 pounds. Standard features included a carrying case, seat, spreaders, air chambers, and either paddles or jointed oars (147). Acme advertised that setup and disassembly required no tools, took only five minutes, and could be done by a novice in the dark. The boat was indeed portable. The carrying case was thirty-six inches long and eight inches wide, and it weighed thirty pounds with the boat packed inside (147).

Most interesting are the little boats' safety features, which Acme advertised as "lifesaving." The company maintained that the boat could not be tipped over by a person standing anywhere on it, and that if filled with water by any cause, even the nine-foot model would hold two people without sinking.

The Acme boat proved popular because it could be transported as luggage on a train, boat, or automobile and was available in many models, including canoes. The sixteen-foot model was adapted for use by the Royal Canadian Mounted Police and was personally used by the governor of the Klondike region. The extensive Acme product line required a fifty-page illustrated catalog (148).

## Steam Launches

Around the same time that Acme folding boats were common in the outer regions of the countryside, the noisy steam launches with pounding pistons and smoky exhausts were churning the waters of the larger lakes. A report of a Michigan fishing experiment circa 1904 pitting an angler in a steam launch against an angler and a powerful oarsman in a sixteen-foot rowboat illuminates how the application of technology to angling affects the number of fish caught.

The objective was to troll the shorelines with spoon lures for muskellunge and compare the number of fish landed by each angler on a daily basis. Both anglers were equipped with identical baitcasting systems, with one exception: the angler aboard the steam launch had ten extra yards of line on the reel spool (149). Many during this time believed that the noise and commotion produced by steam-powered paddle craft had a negative effect on the number of fish caught, and this, multiday test would ferret out the truth.

It comes as no surprise that on a daily basis, the angler in the steam launch covered much more shoreline—five to six miles of shore, plus seven miles to and from the fishing camp—than the rowboat angler, who fished two miles of nearby shore (149). At the end of the contest, the promoters were astonished that the rowboat angler lost: "Not once did he equal the string [of fish] caught by the machine! Whatever may have been the real reason, the rowboat man is now a convert to the motor as a means of propulsion in trolling" (149).

## From Stern-Mounted Engines to Outboard Motors

The report about the Michigan fishing contest noted, "Since that day conditions in boat building have changed materially. Instead of a heavy, awkward steam launch...one can purchase for less than $150 a roomy, broad-beamed, sixteen-foot boat with a motor powerful enough to develop a speed of five miles [per hour]; the whole weighing less than 500 pounds" This boat, used on northern Minnesota rivers had a shallow draft of twelve inches and was powered by a internal stern-mounted gas engine connected to a rear paddle wheel. The manufacturer later replaced this particular model with a "sixteen-foot clinker built launch" that could reach six miles per hour. The newer model had a removable engine that allowed transport of the boat between various locations just like an ordinary rowboat. (149).

Popular for a short period, the use of internally mounted gasoline engines on small fishing boats quickly diminished with the invention of the outboard motor. By the early twentieth century, a variety of outboards existed, all in the 2 to 3½ hp range. The French-manufactured Motogodille appeared in about 1904; it was followed by the Waterman, Evinrude, Lockwood-Ash, Koban, and Caille motors, all competing against each other. The eventual winner was the Evinrude, made by Ole Evinrude, a Norwegian immigrant living in Wisconsin.

## Ole Evinrude, a Good Mechanic and Inventor

Ole, a large, powerful man, had a friend named Bess Cary who enjoyed spending time with him during Sunday outings on the lake. She also enjoyed ice cream. One hot summer Sunday, after Ole had rowed them two and a half miles to an island lake retreat, Bess mentioned that a cold dish of ice cream would be nice. Ole, who was evidently either a good sport or a romantic, rowed back to the town store and returned with the ice cream. (150). While rowing back and forth, he pondered the thought of a small boat motor. Having worked as an apprentice machinist, engine mechanic, toolmaker, and now as a pattern maker in a Milwaukee shop, Ole was inclined to such thoughts.

On a two-week vacation from work, in a little shed workshop he rented, Ole put his ideas to work (150). By December 1910, Motor Boat magazine advertised his outboard motor.

Many of the original outboards could propel rowboats at speeds close to five miles per hour. As early as 1912, Evinrude advertised a top speed of seven miles per hour, a big selling feature (150). Another crowd-pleaser was Ole's automatic reverse that allowed shifting with the engine running, from forward to reverse or vice versa, just by twisting the tiller handle to release a catch and turning the prop 180 degrees (151). Unlike some other outboards, the Evinrude was propeller-guided; the direction of the boat was changed by moving the propeller with the motor's tiller handle. No rudder was necessary (151). Dixie Carroll—an author, sportsman, and it seems an Evinrude fan—wrote in 1919, "I have kicked my Evinrude through weed beds galore, in among the windfalls and rocks, let every old amateur motor running fiend around my camp use it and it still purrs like a happy kitten when it gets the spark" (152).

After making a fortune, Ole Evinrude initially retired in 1913, when his wife Bess became ill. Chris Meyer, his partner, bought Ole's portion of the business. As part of the sale agreement, Evinrude was required to abstain from participating in the outboard motor industry for five years. However, this stipulation did not prevent him from personal research and development. During his industry hiatus, Evinrude developed

Lake Fishing, an illustration by Louis Rhead

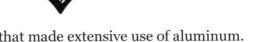

a new twin-cylinder engine that made extensive use of aluminum. The new outboard weighed one-third less than his former company's single-cylinder model and produced 50 percent more horsepower.

In 1920 Ole and Bess were back in business under the trade name Elto, based on the acronym for his former company's engine, the Evinrude Light Twin Outboard. Ole marketed his newly developed engine as the Ruddertwin. Unlike his earlier propeller-guided outboard, this stationary-mounted outboard was steered by a rudder. I find this curious; it seems like a step backward, especially in light of Ole's earlier success over competitors who used a similar rudder steering system. Nevertheless, the conspicuously aluminum appearance and substantially lighter 4 hp Ruddertwin drove Elto sales higher. Ole would need those sales, because competition from a new kid on the block would be furious.

## The Johnson Brothers

Lou Johnson conceived an idea for an outboard motor in 1903 when he had to row an eighteen-foot boat ten miles upstream to harvest walnuts. Luckily for Evinrude, Johnson did not immediately pursue development of a marine motor. In the minds of many, Lou Johnson and his brothers Harry and Julius were the best gasoline engine experts on the face of the planet (153). Rather than putting their talents to work on the outboard, they focused on designing an aircraft motor—a lightweight V4 cylinder, 60 hp, two-cycle engine (154). Because no aircraft was available to test the motor, they built one of the first monoplanes in history; never having seen one, they constructed it from an article in a flight magazine (154).

The Johnsons' aircraft flew for the first time in August 1911, with Lou at the controls. In fact, it flew twice that day, because on the initial flight Lou had to teach himself to fly (154). In those days, other aircraft were biplanes made of wood and fabric; the Johnson brothers' monoplane had a hollow aluminum and nickel steel tail assembly. Despite the excellent innovation, American financial investors failed to recognize the merits of the project, and it remained unfunded. In 1957 the Johnson brothers were still alive when their contribution to aviation history reached Paul Garber, head curator of the Aviation Museum at the Smithsonian, who persuaded Lou Johnson to produce a one-tenth scale model of their plane; it remains on exhibit there today (154).

In 1922 Lou, Harry, and Julius Johnson produced the most revolutionary outboard motor of the period. After concluding that single-cylinder engines turned the crankshaft too slowly and did not develop power to full potential, they fixed that shortcoming with a twin-cylinder high-speed engine. Lew Johnson designed a 2 hp, water-cooled outboard motor named the Light Twin; its thirty-five pound weight was about half that of the other rowboat motors of the day (153). The price was $140, and 3,324 units sold in the first year (153). The consensus of mechanical authorities who examined the motor was that because of the low weight, it would not be durable enough to withstand the high revolutions per minute it turned out, but Lew Johnson proved that they were wrong. The engines Johnson sold to thousands of happy customers demonstrated that low weight and mechanical durability are not necessarily incompatible.

## Outboard Motors Affect Hull Design

The outboard motor offered several benefits to anglers. It allowed a solo angler to easily troll the shorelines without assistance. With fish concentrated in fertile water, the outboard provided a fast means past the vacant zones; and when bad weather approached, anglers could return to dock with much greater expediency.

Early on, only two types of watercraft employed the outboard: the canoe, appropriately modified with a square stern, and the rowboat. This was about to change. Johnson's new high-speed outboard made it necessary to rethink hull design, an endeavor that began in earnest during the mid-1920s.

By the late 1920s, three types of small boat hulls were generally available. Each had specific advantages.

- *Round-bottom hulls* were very strong, like a barrel, and fairly fast. However, they were the least laterally stable and tended to roll.

- *V-bottom hulls* were strong like a crate, but not as strong as a barrel. They were generally stable.

- *Flat-bottom hulls* were cheap and strong. They were the most stable, possibly the fastest, and rarely capsized, although they did tend to skid during turns.

The arc-bottom hull, also available at the time, was primarily a racing hull (150).

By comparing the characteristics of the three hull designs, it becomes apparent why many small fishing boats employed flat bottoms. However, innovative anglers would seek improvements.

## The Skeeter Bass Boat

In 1948 Holmes Thurman of Louisiana, frustrated by having flat-bottomed boats blown around by the wind, innovated boat design by building the first bass boat (155). Thurman's approach was to keep the flat-bottom, hard-chine design and employ a moderately raked bow for speed, because the shallow-draft hull worked well in the cypress-filled lakes of northwest Louisiana. To mitigate wind, he reduced the surface area of the freeboards by employing a tumblehome hull design, thereby turning the freeboards into inward-sloped side decks from the waterline to the gunwales. This maximized the beam at the waterline to gain additional lateral stability. The inward sloping sides of the boat's superstructure now formed a narrow, box-shaped interior with ample storage space along the edges of the boat floor (155). Fitted with a long, skinny bow, Thurman's molded plywood boat resembled a mosquito, so it was given the name Skeeter. It was fast, stable, and easy to paddle.

Fiberglass-reinforced boat hulls, first produced in 1944 (131), made a timely appearance and were a major enhancement for the previously wooden Skeeter (156). One of the first mass-produced fiberglass boats was initially manufactured in Marshall, Texas, and marketed by Reeves Marine in Shreveport, Louisiana (156). The name Skeeter was retained as the brand.

Stemco, a manufacturing company based in Longview, Texas, purchased Skeeter in 1961. Stemco sold two different models of the Skeeter bass boat: the C-1350, the original 13½-foot model; and the C-1500, a fifteen-foot model called the Super Skeeter. With a transom constructed of plywood and fiberglass and laminated to withstand motor stress, the C-1500 rated for a 35 hp outboard motor and three passengers. The C-1350 rated for two passengers and 25 hp (157).

Over the years following the invention of the original Skeeter, hundreds of other manufacturers have produced many variations of the type. The modern bass boat, specifically designed for two or three anglers, is sleek and low, has an open-cockpit design, and provides casting platforms at the bow and stern. Matched with a high-powered outboard motor, these speedsters can cover a lot of water in a short time and are rigged to support the hunt. Most have an array of equipment, such as a bow-mounted electric trolling motor, a live well with oxygenated water, a GPS system, sonar, and even beverage coolers. In 2016 Skeeter Performance Fishing offered three variations of their bass boat; the largest, the ZX-250, was twenty feet, ten inches long and rated for 250 hp.

The original Skeeter Bass Boat, Courtesy of the History of Fishing Museum, Branson, MO

## Multispecies Trailer Boats

In 1946, just two years before Thurman invented the bass boat, the multispecies small aluminum boat, the workhorse of the fleet, received significant impetus. These small, lightweight, durable trailer boats, powered by outboard engines, offered both tiller and remote steering options. Three Minnesota boat builders contributed to their development.

*Paul Larson*

Following World War II, Paul Larson, founder of Larson Boat Works in Little Falls, Minnesota, started producing aluminum fishing boats. Apparently Robert H. Wold, a military veteran who had gained experience with aluminum aircraft applications during the war, presented an idea for constructing aluminum boats to Larson, who saw merit in it (158). Accordingly, Larson formed a separate company called Larson Watercraft, and Wold served as secretary-treasurer and general manager.

In 1946, in one of its initial shipments from the new production facility, the company sent forty twelve-foot boats to an Idaho dealer. In 1954 Larson entered the molded fiberglass boat business, and this new product line would eventually dominate his manufacturing business. One of the popular Larson boat models, the Crestliner, had a name with a nice ring to it, and this became the company's new moniker (158). In 2004 Brunswick, a company famous for billiard tables, acquired Crestliner Boats.

## G. Howard Lund

Another innovative Minnesota boat builder was G. Howard Lund (no one called him Gordon). Lund built his first boat out of galvanized steel in 1939, and in his words, "It was crude but it was all mine!" (159). In 1947 Lund constructed an aluminum duck boat. Very proud of the workmanship used, he was prone to carrying the new boat on the top of his car as he drove around the small town of New York Mills, Minnesota. One lucky day, a representative for Inland Marine Corporation saw Howard's boat and asked him if he would consider building more. Howard answered yes and got an immediate order for fifty duck boats (159). Thus began Lund Boat Company.

By 1957 Lund employed fifteen workers and a distributor in St. Paul. The business grew quickly, and in 1961 Lund reincorporated the company as Lund Metal Craft. That same year, Howard acquired the well-respected Shell Lake Boat Company of Wisconsin, a builder since 1904; thus he expanded into the fiberglass market. Lund increased versatility with the new product line, and the company continued to grow over the next eleven years. By 1972 Lund had opened a manufacturing facility in Steinbach, Manitoba. When Lund died in 2003, the company had 250 dealers in the United States, 120 in Canada, and two in Europe. The main manufacturing plant in New York Mills had 575 employees, and 150 more worked at the Canadian plant (160).

## Alumacraft Boat Company

Located in St. Peter, Minnesota, Alumacraft Boat Company built its first aluminum boat in 1946. In 2012 the company was purchased by Corinthian Capital Group LLC, a private equity firm. Using the company's 2016 online Boat Builder pricing and options guide, an angler could choose between sixteen different boat models and 112 variations—quite a generous assortment.

# Angling Kayaks

For the physically active, environmentally conscious angler, the oldest yet newest choice is the human-powered craft. In the late twentieth century, new types of human-powered boats became available, increasing the number of hip-boot baitcasters with access to waterborne craft. Kayaks with leg-powered flippers or propellers, specifically outfitted for angling, are the trend in certain environments. Easy to store and transport, they provide comfort, casting platforms for seated or standing use, speeds up to four miles per hour, decent storage, and good exercise. These modern angling kayaks sprang from the inventive minds of two young men.

### Ketterman and Czarnowski

As young boys, Greg Ketterman and his brother Dan would test "model sailboats by holding the mast in one hand and the clew in the other, then swing the mast. . . . As the sail twisted it looked like a propeller blade and would produce thrust" (161). Greg also played on an air mattress in the pool, propelling himself by moving his arms from the elbow down and varying the angle of attack of his hands in the water to produce thrust. These early experiences helped the brothers develop innovative ideas about how to propel watercraft. By the 1980s the two brothers developed the TriFoiler sailboat, and in 1993 their boat set a new world speed record of 43.6 knots (50.17 miles per hour) (161).

Greg Ketterman's interest in wind propulsion and the effect of thrust on boat hulls no doubt led him to keep abreast of new technology developments at the Massachusetts Institute of Technology (MIT), where a young student, James Czarnowski, was leading the way. Czarnowski, like Ketterman, had been interested in marine propulsion systems since his childhood. "I've been building strange little boats like this since I was eight years old," he said in a 1997 interview. "My first one was a papier-mâché paddle-wheel boat with a small electric motor that powered a popsicle-stick paddle wheel. Now that I'm at MIT, I can build more advanced models" (162).

In 1996, at the New England Aquarium in Boston, Czarnowski spent six months observing how penguins swam using fin propulsion to propel their bodies through the water with speed and efficiency. Following his investigation, Czarnowski spent another six months building a fin-powered prototype boat in order to win MIT approval to continue the project, which he named Proteus. In March 1997, Czarnowski took his prototype

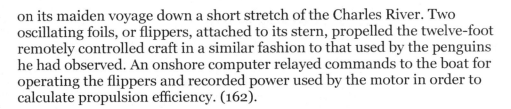

on its maiden voyage down a short stretch of the Charles River. Two oscillating foils, or flippers, attached to its stern, propelled the twelve-foot remotely controlled craft in a similar fashion to that used by the penguins he had observed. An onshore computer relayed commands to the boat for operating the flippers and recorded power used by the motor in order to calculate propulsion efficiency. (162).

Greg Ketterman, who had been experimenting with similar propulsion systems, immediately turned his attention to Czarnowski and hired him as director of engineering at Hobie Cat Company, where Ketterman was the vice president of engineering. At the beach at Oceanside, California, in 1997, Ketterman introduced a propulsion system called the Mirage Drive that incorporated the new fins. Kayaking would never be the same. On February 8, 2000, Ketterman was awarded US Patent 6,022,249 A for a watercraft powered by those fins. The patent claims that "each of said flappers is carried by a mast with each of said flappers being sufficiently rotatable about said mast so that the flapper produces forward thrust with respect to the longitudinal dimension of said watercraft while moving in both directions along said arcuate [curved] path." Ketterman and Czarnowski continued inventing together, assigning patent rights to Hobie Cat.

The angling kayaks, propelled by pedaling, are feature-laden platforms from twelve to seventeen feet in length. The twelve-foot version with a five-hundred-pound load capacity has a thirty-six-inch beam and weighs 129 pounds fully rigged. The easily removable propulsion system consists of a set of adjustable pedals connected to two fins that flex from side to side. The fins create pitch and propulsion and drive the craft at about four miles per hour. The craft employs a retractable rudder with a simple left-handed rudder control lever and is fitted with highly adjustable, comfortable seating. Included among the standard angling features are rod holders, tackle storage, a transducer mounting, and cable routing for fish finders. Optional features include an eight-gallon live well, an electric motor, and a power pole automatic anchor system, a novel and surprisingly effortless way to set and retract an anchor while seated.

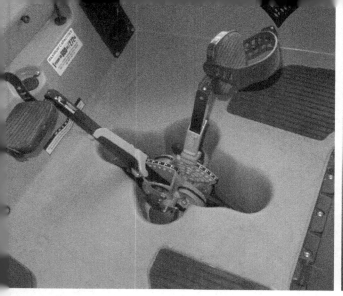

Hobie Mirage Drive installed (left) and removed for display (right)

## Conclusion

Since the inception of the sport, the options for baitcasting watercraft have increased dramatically. The variety of boats, canoes, kayaks, and flotation devices available to twenty-first-century anglers is truly remarkable. Because aluminum boats typically have a very long service life, many are available as previously owned watercraft. A thorough inspection and a negotiated price often lead to new angling adventures.

Trolling with live bait, an illustration by Louis Rhead

From his book, *Lake and Stream Game Fishing*, author Dixie Carroll displays his 12-pound walleye.

# Chapter 14

# EXPANDING THE POSSIBILITIES

## No Angling Absolutes except Change

King Charles I—like his father, King James I—believed he could grade British sporting behaviors as worthy or unworthy of his approval, restrict practice to only approved sports, and demand that the permitted sports be practiced on Sundays. That belief, however, proved lethal, because circumstances had changed since his father's time. By the 1640s, powerful religious forces in Britain already had decided that Charles was dead wrong. Other than productive activities—hawking, hunting, fowling, and fishing—the Puritans believed that no sport was worthy of practice on Sunday.

Reminiscent of the two English kings, some Americans have thought it possible to determine the worthiness of the sport of others. Since the days of the well-intentioned sports writers of the mid-1800s, who appealed to one's character while attempting to develop a sport angling code, other sincere individuals have also tried to define respectable angling. An actual case in point, possibly one of the most egregious, surfaced during the early 1950s following the introduction of the angling method called spinning. The resulting controversy escalated to involve anglers across the United States.

## Spinning and Spincasting

Bache Hamilton Brown, an architect who had spent significant time fishing in England, learned the spinning method there. Pioneered in Europe around 1900, the method had proven highly effective, so Brown brought it to America in 1932. Initially it failed to generate interest among anglers. Brown returned from another trip to England with examples of spinning reels, line, lures, and the specifications to produce rods, but the looming world war put his project on hold until 1946 (163).

At the war's end, many of the sixteen million American veterans became anglers. Spinning proved effective and spread quickly, even though appropriate spinning tackle, initially supplied by importers rather

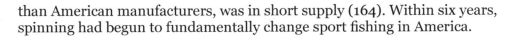

than American manufacturers, was in short supply (164). Within six years, spinning had begun to fundamentally change sport fishing in America.

Humans do not universally accept change, and some anglers viewed spinning askance. Excessive marketing of the sport, along with rumors that spinning made it too easy to catch fish, sent some well-intentioned guardians of sport fishing into panic mode. Disagreements between members of popular rod and gun clubs of the day created animosity toward spinning; their board members hurriedly passed propositions judging the spinning method as unworthy of sport. Consequently, spinning was banned in certain American waters (164), and the rumor mill spat out many absolute definitions of what constitutes worthy sport. According to Robert Page Lincoln, the most insidious tale circulated nationally declared that spinning was putting America's fish population in jeopardy of extinction (102).

In 1954 Ray Ovington, in his book *Spinning in America*, predicted that the attitude toward spinning would eventually change with "the passing of time and perfection and general acceptance of the tackle" (164). He believed that spinning would become a highly regarded sport fishing method. He was right. Baitcasting relinquished its popularity to spinning because many anglers, especially novices, preferred the new, easy to operate, backlash-free spinning reel capable of casting very light lures. Spinning became the recognized American solution for employing lighter line, finesse techniques, and ultralight angling. Soon it became known as a viable alternative to other angling methods. Additionally, most spinning systems were able to cast any lure in the tackle box.

In 1949, within three years of its American start-up, spinning spawned another new angling method that advertised backlash-free operation: spincasting. The newest method offered a high level of utility and single-handed operation that served the needs of many anglers. It proved an excellent way for novices to learn to fish, and for the occasional angler there was often no reason to switch to other methods.

The advent of spinning and spincasting increased the number of American sport angling methods from three to five, the number that remain today. Listed chronologically by date of origin in America, these angling methods are still-fishing (circa 1612), fly-fishing (circa 1784), baitcasting (circa 1815), spinning (1946), and spincasting (1949).

# The Baitcasting Reel, an Alternative for Some Anglers

Spinning and spincasting reels did not always meet the specific needs of avid anglers targeting multiple fish species, especially those having heavy body weights and/or sharp teeth capable of breaking or cutting the lighter monofilament lines. The go-to alternative was the casting reel that Snyder originally designed to meet angling requirements for the powerful river fish of Kentucky: muskellunge, walleye pike, and the smallmouth variety of the black bass. Formidable game fish such as these require rugged reels capable of accurately casting at all distances with a wide range of lure types and weights—often requiring heavier lines, sometimes using cut-proof steel-wire leaders.

The need for this type of reel has remained strong into the twenty-first century. The modern mechanical descendants of Snyder's reel satisfy anglers like no other; they are the finest tools available for powerful game fish. Many individuals keep casting systems as a backup for use when spinning tackle is not up to the job; they are good tools to hold in reserve for badass fish. Beyond that, other anglers see huge possibilities for the old veteran multiplier.

## New Tackle, New Capability, More Fun

Generally, during the period between the two world wars, little development in the baitcasting method occurred. The large-lure systems used by the majority of anglers remained unsophisticated and much less effective than what could have been developed (165). However, some anglers did envision finer, lighter, smaller tackle that could improve the sport of baitcasting—an activity anglers referred to as "plugging," because of the plug-shaped wooden lures they cast.

In Harrisburg, Pennsylvania, an astute cadre of anglers led by Charlie Fox dedicated themselves to increasing the knowledge and advancement of the plugging sport by using a smaller lure and lighter tackle. They called the refined sport "midget plugging." In 1944 Alfred W. Miller (Sparse Grey Hackle) predicted that the future progress of angling in America might well rest on the work of Fox's angling group. Six years later, Miller said that his prediction had already been justified, because midget plugging had become a new sport, "one as subtle and delicate and capable of future development as dry-fly angling" (165).

Baitcasting was on the cusp of transitioning into something better. Segments of the American public were practicing baitcasting with light-spooled casting reels, lightweight line, longer rods, and small lures (102). Further improving the situation was the availability of new American-manufactured small lures made possible by the advent of spinning. These lures were a welcomed addition to the baitcasting system because they brought new functionality, thereby making baitcasting better than it had been.

In the twenty-first-century, the angling method for skillfully and accurately presenting light lures weighing from 1/16 to ¼ ounce is known by various names. These include finesse fishing, the baitcast finesse system, light-line fishing, and light-lure casting. Because the term "finesse" is not specifically associated with any particular angling method or equipment size, and because the fundamental purpose is to cast a light lure, I will call it "light-lure casting" from here on.

Whatever it's called, the light-lure casting system, although one of the most significant sport angling improvements in many years, originally had less effect on angling in general than it would have if spinning had not doused it with cold water. However, it was not dead. By 1955 it had become popular in the baitcasting community, and tackle manufacturers greatly increased their lightweight casting products as a hedge against the use of spinning gear.

The new tackle proved perfect for the innovative and growing technique of light-lure casting (166). According to Ernest Liotta Jr., a national champion in bait and fly casting, typical baitcasting lures produced before 1950 weighed between 3/8 and 3/4 ounce (167). In the early 1950s, Charlie Fox's belief that ¼-ounce lures were the most effective for angling became widely accepted. Consequently, lure weights between 3/16 and 5/16 ounce became the norm for light-lure casting.

Documented in 1950 as a baitcasting technique using specialized (hot-rodded) tackle, light-lure casting has been in continuous American angling practice for over sixty-five years, and it is one heck of a lot of fun. The technique has great potential to gain more traction with anglers if manufacturers could meet the same challenge that they did in 1930: find ways to lower the cost of appropriate reels.

Nevertheless, baitcasting is no longer the primary tool for non-tournament angling as it was in the first half of the twentieth century. While some might think this is a sad commentary on where baitcasting has gone, others believe it reveals a possibility for expanding rather than limiting the sport. Since 1976, because of the overwhelming support long exhibited by anglers for each of these sport fishing methods, the official rules for tackle and equipment in Bassmaster tournaments have allowed all three methods: baitcasting, spincasting, and spinning. Each of these methods remains the finest tool available for its designed purpose.

## Possibilities

Baitcasting became a reality because of many innovations across the decades: Snyder's multiplying reel and its continued development in Kentucky; Henshall's *Book of the Black Bass* and his documented fishing method; Acme's folding boat; Buel's spoon lure; Creme's plastic worm and the unknown anglers' Texas method of rigging it; and so on, ad infinitum. Anglers are an inventive bunch; they recognize possibilities and take action to make the sport better. Making the most of those possibilities is the finest anyone can do.

An illustration by Louis Rhead

# Works Cited

1. King James. *King's Maiesties Declaration To His Subjects Concerning Lawful Sports To Be Used.* London: Bonham Norton and John Bill, Deputie Printers for the King's most Excellent Maiestie, 1618. Reprinted with added commentary by Benj. Ashworth, 22 South Fourth St., Philadelphia, 1866.

2. Harvey, I. M. W. "Poaching and Sedition in Fifteenth-Century England." In *Lordship and Learning: Studies in Memory of Trevor Auston,* ed. by Ralph Evans. Woodbridge: Boydell Press, 2004.

3. Henshall, James A. *Book of the Black Bass.* Cincinnati: Robert Clarke, 1889, p. 66.

4. Walker, Williston. *A History of the Christian Church.* 3rd ed. (revised by Robert T. Handy, Union Theological Seminary, NY). New York: Charles Scribner's Sons, 1970. ISBN 684-41471-6. Library of Congress catalog no. 70-108358. Standard history volume for Anglican Seminary students by the professor of Ecclesiastical History, Yale University.

5. Goodspeed, Charles Eliot. *Angling in America: Its Early History and Literature.* Boston: Houghton Mifflin Company, 1939.

6. Johnson, Karl E. "Problematizing Puritan Play." *Leisure.* 2009. Vol. 33, pp. 31–54.

7. Cornell, Martyn. "A Short History of Bottled Beer." *Zythophile* blog [online]. January 15, 2010. [Accessed November 8, 2016.] http://zythophile. co.uk/2010/01/15/a-short-history-of-bottled-beer. The author is a beer educator, beer consultant, journalist, and beer historian, and won awards from the British Guild of Beer Writers five years running, 2011–15.

8. "The Puritans and Sports." *Beacon Street Diary* blog, Congregational Library & Archives [online]. February 28, 2014. [Accessed November 7, 2016.] http://www.congregationallibrary.org/blog/201402/ puritans-and-sport.

9. Riess, Steven A. *Sports in America from Colonial Times to the Twenty-First Century: An Encyclopedia.* Vol. 1. London and New York: Routledge, Taylor & Francis Group, 2011, p. 351. ISBN 978-0-7656-1706-4.

10. Koller, Larry. *The Treasury of Angling.* New York: Golden Press, 1963, pp. 22, 32, 32, 159, 25.

11. Sparse Grey Hackle (pseud. of Alfred W. Miller). "Only Yesterday." In *Great Fishing Tackle Catalogs of the Golden Age,* ed. by Samuel Melner and Herman Kessler. New York: Crown Publishers, 1972.

12. Watson, John Fanning, and Hazard, Willis P. *Annals of Philadelphia and Pennsylvania in the Olden Time*. Vol. 3. Philadelphia: Edwin S. Stuart, 1877, pp. 291, 294.

13. Barlow, Elizabeth. "New York: A Once and Future Arcadia." *New York* magazine. November 29, 1971, p. 53.

14. *Minutes of the Common Council of the City of New York*. Vol. 4. New York: Dodd, Mead, 1905, p. 209.

15. Hayward, Fred C. "History of Sir John Johnson." *United Empire Loyalists' Association of Canada* [online]. http://www.uelac.org/Sir-JohnJohnson/SirJohnJohnson.php.

16. Simms, Jeptha R. *Trappers of New York*. Albany: C. Munsell, 1850, pp. 31–41.

17. Pearsall, Glen. "Fish House: Great Sacandaga Lake's Underwater Mysteries." *Adirondack Almanack* [online]. August 17, 2015. [Accessed September 3, 2015.] http://www.adirondackalmanack.com/2015/08/fish-house-great-sacandaga-lakes-underwater-mysteries.html.

18. Stone, William L. *The Life and Times of Sir William Johnson, Bart.* Vol. 2. Albany: J. Munsell, 1865, pp. 163, 164.

19. Hunter, Robert Jr. *Quebec to Carolina in 1785–1786: Being the travel diary and observations of Robert Hunter, Jr., a young merchant of London.* Edited by Louis B. Wright and Marion Tinling. San Marino: Huntington Library, 1943, pp. 63–66.

20. "The Economic Crisis of the 1780s." *U.S. History: Pre-Columbian to the New Millennium* [online]. http://www.ushistory.org/us/14d.asp.

21. Price, Alexa. "Mount Vernon Fisheries." *George Washington Digital Encyclopedia* [online]. 2016. [Accessed November 7, 2016.] http://www.mountvernon.org/digital-encyclopedia/article/mount-vernon-fisheries.

22. Hamby, Alonzo L. *Outline of U.S. History*. New York: Nova Science Publishers, 2007. Chapter 5, "Westward Expansion and Regional Differences." Available at http://iipdigital.usembassy.gov/media/pdf/books/historytln.pdf.

23. "The Treaty of Sycamore Shoals." *A History of the Daniel Boone National Forest, 1770–1970* [online]. [Accessed March 18, 2015.] http://www.foresthistory.org/ASPNET/Publications/region/8/daniel_boone/chap8.htm.

24. US Census Bureau, 1790, 1800.

25. Sole, Jeff. Email exchanges with Emmett Babler. March 25, 2015. Sole was the Director of Conservation Programs at The Nature Conservancy.

26. Wilber Smith Associates. *Kentucky Water Transportation Corridors Public Riverport Development and Intermodal Access*. Transportation Cabinet, Commonwealth of Kentucky, 2000.

27. "Kentucky Native Fish." *The Nature Conservancy* [online]. 2015. [Accessed March 25, 2015.] http://www.nature.org/ourinitiatives/ regions/northamerica/unitedstates/kentucky/explore/kentuckys-na-tive-fish-1.xml.

28. Smith, Zachariah F. *The History of Kentucky*. Louisville: Prentice Press, 1895.

29. Henshall, James A. *Book of the Black Bass*. Cincinnati: Robert Clarke, 1881.

30. ———. "The Angling Exhibit of the World's Columbian Exposition." In *The Sportsman's Directory and Year Book*. 3rd annual ed. New York: Pond and Goldey, 1893, pp. 9–14.

31. Hart, David. "What Bass Eat." *Bassmaster* [online]. November 2, 2016. http://www.bassmaster.com/what-bass-eat.

32. Henshall, James A. *More About the Black Bass*. Cincinnati: Robert Clarke, 1889.

33. Natural Resources Conservation Service. *Plant Guide: Giant Cane, Arundinaria gigantea Muhl*. Washington, DC: US Department of Agriculture.

34. Henshall, James A. *Book of the Black Bass: New Edition Revised and Extended*. Cincinnati: Robert Clarke, 1904, pp. 190, 190, 192, 191, 196, 196, 193, 199, 197.

35. Ustonson, Onesimus. *The True Art of Angling*. London: n.p., 1770.

36. Vernon, Steven K. *Antique Fishing Reels*. Harrisburg, PA: Stackpole Books, 1985, p. 14. ISBN 0-8117-0108-5.

37. Stewart, Frank M., III. "G. Ustonson: Reelmaker to His Majesty." *Antique Angler*. March/April 1984. Vol. 5, p. 1. *Antique Angler*, PO Box K, Stockton, NJ 08559.

38. Lincoln, Robert Page. "The Kentucky Reel." *Field and Stream.* March 1930. Vol. 11, pp. 26, 27, 77.

39. Henshall, James A. "The Autobiography of the Apostle of the Black Bass, Father of the Grayling and Dean of American Anglers." Ninth Paper. *Forest and Stream.* January 1920. Vol. 90, pp. 18, 19, 34, 36.

40. ———. "Evolution of the Kentucky Reel." *Outing.* December 1900. Vol. 37, no. 3, pp. 288–293.

41. "History of the Kentucky Reel." *Forest and Stream.* January 1915. Vol. 84, no. 1, pp. 26, 27.

42. Henshall, James A. "More About the Kentucky Reel." *Forest and Stream.* February 1915, p. 82.

43. "The Fishing Reel: A Talk with the Veteran Maker, B. F. Meek." *Frankfort Roundabout.* April 13, 1895. Interview with Meek.

44. McClane, A. J. "My Old Kentucky Reel." *Field and Stream.* January 1953.

45. Vernon, Steven K., and Stewart, Frank M., III. *Fishing Reel Makers of Kentucky.* Plano: Thomas B. Reel, 1992. ISBN 96-20155-3-9.

46. Hatter, Russel. Interview with Emmett Babler, September 2016. Personal discovery by Mr. Hatter of the Capital City Museum, Frankfort, while researching cemetery records.

47. Marston, Barry L. *The Ayres Family of Owen County, Kentucky.* Frankfort, KY: self-published e-book, 2007.

48. Silversmith Directory. *Sterling Flatware Fashions and Facts* [online]. [Accessed March 11, 2015.] http://sterlingflatwarefashions.com/Silver-smiths/SSA4.html.

49. "Reel-Maker Meek to Retire From Business." *Louisville (KY) Courier-Journal.* September 11, 1898, p. B8.

50. B. C. Milam & Son. *The Milam, The Genuine and Original "Frankfort" "Kentucky" Reel.* Frankfort, KY: n.p., post-1900. Catalog that includes information about the history of the reel and reel maker.

51. Meek, J. F., and Frankfort, B. F. Letter to Mr. Fletcher regarding payment of two notes. December 8, 1840.

52. Parish, Charles E., and Johnson, Leland R. *Engineering the Kentucky River: The Commonwealth's Waterway*. US Army Corps of Engineers, Louisville District, 1999. TC425.K43 J65 1999.

53. Engstrom, Kadie. "Steamboats and the Ohio River." Available from Related Instructional Resources section, *Electronic Field Trip to the Belle of Louisville* [online]. 2017. [Accessed February 27, 2017.] https://www.ket.org/education/resources/electronic-field-trip-belle-louisville/.

54. Stewart, Frank M., III. "J. L. Sage." *Antique Angler*. September/October 1984, p. 14. Antique Angler, PO Box K, Stockton, NJ 08559.

55. Connelley, William Elsey, and Coulter, E. M. *History of Kentucky*. Vol. 5. Edited by Charles Kerr. Chicago and New York: American Historical Society, 1922, pp. 174, 175.

56. B. C. Milam & Son. *The Milam Frankfort Kentucky Fishing Reel*. Frankfort, KY: n.p., post-1915. Catalog.

57. US Department of the Interior, National Park Service. "History & Culture." *John H. Chaffee Blackstone River Valley* [online]. March 20, 2015. http://www.nps.gov/blac/learn/historyculture/index.htm.

58. University of Vermont. "19th Century Water Powered Factories." *Landscape Change Program* [online]. 2011. [Accessed March 9, 2015.] http://www.uvm.edu/landscape/dating/industrial_architecture/early_factory.php.

59. Carini, Frank. "Environmental News for Southern New England." *ecoRI News* [online]. December 18, 2010. www.ecori.org/pollution-contamination/2010/12/18/ris.

60. Robinson, Robert V., and Briggs, Carl M. "The Rise of Factories in Nineteenth-Century Indianapolis." *American Journal of Sociology*. Nov. 1991. Vol. 97, no. 3, p. 622.

61. Waterman, Charles F. *Fishing in America*. New York: Holt, Rinehart and Winston, 1975, p. 27.

62. Roosevelt, Theodore. "The Great Leap Westward" was a favorite Roosevelt saying regarding nineteenth-century US westward expansion.

63. "The Importance of the West." *U.S. History: Pre-Columbian to the New Millennium* [online]. http://www.ushistory.org/us/21a.asp.

64. "The Gold Rush of 1849." *History* [online]. http://www.history.com/topics/gold-rush-of-1849.

65. Barnet, Harry E. "Kentucky's Westminster Abbey: State Cemetery at Frankfort a Show Place." *The Dearborn Independent*. October 7, 1922.

66. Whisman, Eric. Interview with John Downs. June 30, 2015. John Downs, of the Capital City Museum in Frankfort, KY, contacted Eric Whisman, a preservation and history professional, and relayed the information to Emmett Babler in an email.

67. Wiley, Edwin, and Rines, Irving E. (eds.). *The United States: Its Beginnings, Progress and Modern Development*. Vol. 6. New York: American Educational Alliance, 1913, pp. 317–319.

68. Norris, Thaddeus. *The American Angler's Book*. Philadelphia: Porter & Coates, 1864.

69. Chubb, Thomas H. "Fishing Tackle, Rods, Reels, Ferrules." In *Great Fishing Tackle Catalogs of the Golden Age*, ed. by Samuel Melner and Hermann Kessler. New York: Crown Publishers, 1972. Pre-1890 catalog published within a book section.

70. Melner, Samuel, and Kessler, Herman, eds. *Great Fishing Tackle Catalogs of the Golden Age*. New York: Crown Publishers, 1972. Introduction and commentary by Sparse Grey Hackle.

71. Gayle, Clarence. "Hand-Made Reels." *The Sporting Goods Dealer*. May 1905. Vol. 12, no. 2, pp. 10–12.

72. Brown, John J. *The Angler's Almanac for 1848*. New York: John J. Brown & Co., 1848.

73. ——. *The American Angler's Guide*. 2nd ed. New York: Burgess, Stringer and Company, 1846.

74. Roosevelt, Robert B. *Superior Fishing*. New York: Carlton, 1865.

75. Carter, Arlan. *19th Century Fishing Lures*. Paducah, KY: Collector Books (division of Schroeder Publishing), 2000.

76. Thompson, Harvey W. *The Spooners*. Dearborn, MI: Eppinger Manufacturing Company, 1979.

77. Roosevelt, Robert B. *Game Fish of the Northern States of America*. New York: Carlton, 1862.

78. Scott, Genio C. *Fishing in American Waters*. Secaucus, NJ: Castle Books, 1989. ISBN 1-55521-516-5. Reproduction of a book originally published in 1875.

79. Wetzel, Charles M. *American Fishing Books*. Stone Harbor, NJ: Meadow Run Press, 1999. ISBN 0-9620609-2-5.

80. Silverside. "Bass and Bass Fishing." *Porter's Spirit of the Times*. March 21, 1857. Vol. 2, no. 3 (whole no. 29), p. 38.

81. Holberton, Wakeman. *The Art of Angling*. New York: Dick and Fitzgerald, 1887.

82. "Site History." *Liberty Hall Historic Site* [online]. [Accessed August 23, 2015.] http://www.libertyhall.org/about/site-history.

83. Stevens, Walter B. *Missouri: The Center State, 1821–1915*. Vol. 2. Chicago-St. Louis: S. J. Clarke, 1915, p. 725.

84. Mares, Bill. *Fishing with the Presidents*. Mechanicsburg, PA: Stackpole Books, 1999. ISBN 0-8117-0638-9.

85. Muntz, Charlie. ""Capturing Henry Clay: Through a Year of the Days of His Life." *Henry Clay* [online]. [Accessed August 23, 2015.] http://henryclay.org/wp-content/uploads/2016/02/Henry-Clay-Calendar1.pdf.

86. Muntz, Charlie, and Davis, Jerrye. "Henry Clay's Travels, 1830–1852." *Henry Clay* [online]. [Accessed August 23, 2015.] http://henryclay.org/wp-content/uploads/2016/02/Henry-Clays-Travels.pdf.

87. Van Buren, Martin. "Autobiography of Martin Van Buren." In *Annual Report of the American Historical Association for the Year 1918*, Vol. 2, ed. by John C. Fitzpatrick. Washington, DC: Government Printing Office, 1919.

88. Cooney, John Ward. "My Recollections of Ex-President Martin Van Buren and His Friends." Parts 1–11. *Annual Publication of the Historical Society of Southern California*. January 1, 1912. Vol. 9. ISSN 21629145.

89. Henshall, James A. Advertisement for subscription sale of *Book of the Black Bass. Forest and Stream*. April 28, 1881. Vol. 16, no. 13, p. 261. Book available May 1, 1881, by previous subscription.

90. Herbert, Henry William. *Fish and Fishing of the United States and British Provinces of North America*. New York: Stringer & Townsend, 1850.

91. Oliver Gibbs, Jr. *Lake Pepin Fish-Chowder: Letters to General Spinner*. New York: H. D. McIntyre & Co., 1869.

92. Holmquist, June Drenning. "Fishing in the Land of 10,00 Lakes." In *Minnesota History*. St. Paul: Minnesota Historical Society, 1953, pp. 252–259.

93. Game and Fish Commission of Minnesota. *First Annual Report of the Game and Fish Commission of Minnesota*. St. Paul, MN: Harrison and Smith Printers, 1892. Minnesota Department of Natural Resources control no. 22 0318 00002 6627.

94. Hallock, Charles. *The Fishing Tourist: Angler's Guide and Reference Book*. New York: Harper & Brothers, Franklin Square, 1873.

95. Baldwin, Roger S. Letter to Theodore Roosevelt. October 28, 1903. *Theodore Roosevelt Center at Dickinson State University* [online]. [Accessed March 29, 2016.] http://www.theodorerooseveltcenter.org/en/Research/Digital-Library/Record.aspx?libID=042557.

96. U.S. Fish and Wildlife Service. *Strategic Plan for the U.S. Fish and Wildlife Service Fish and Aquatic Conservation Program: FY 2016–2020*. 2015. Available at https://www.fws.gov/fisheries/pdf_files/FAC_StrategyPlan_2016-2020.pdf.

97. Hough, Emerson. "Angling in the Middle West." *Outing*. August 1901. Vol. 38, no. 5.

98. Grissom, Herbert. "The Black Bass and Some Sportsmen." *Outing*. May 1915. Vol. 66, p. 183.

99. Henshall, James A. *Book of the Black Bass*. New Edition, Revised and Re-Written. New York: Appleton-Century Company, 1939.

100. Netherton, Cliff. *History of the Sport of Casting: People, Events, Records, Tackle and Literature, Early Times*. Lakeland: American Casting Foundation, 1981. ISBN 0-96-05960-1-1.

101. Smith, O. W. *Casting Tackle and Methods*. Cincinnati: Stewart & Kidd Company, 1920, p. 5.

102. Lincoln, Robert Page. *Black Bass Fishing*. Harrisburg, PA: Stackpole, 1952.

103. Netherton, Cliff. *History of the Sport of Casting: Golden Years*. Lakeland: American Casting Foundation, 1983. ISBN 0-9605960-3-8.

104. Shakespeare, William Jr. *The Art of Baitcasting*. Kalamazoo: Wm. Shakespeare Jr. Company. Published as part of a tackle catalog, 1902.

105. Darling, Lou S. *Tournament Casting and the Proper Equipment*. New York: J. Cliff Blanchard, 1907.

106. Arbogast, Fred. "Distance Bait Reels." *The Scientific Angler*. March 1924.

107. Ripley, Ozark (pseud. of John Baptiste de Macklot Thompson). *Modern Bait & Fly Casting*. New York & London: D. Appleton, 1928. In memory of Emerson Hough.

108. Lamb, Jack. *How to Catch Game Fish*. Fort Worth, TX: Jack Lamb, 1937.

109. Stinson, Sam S. "Whence the Plug?" *The American Angler*. May 1918.

110. Heddon, W. T. "Bait Casting in Florida, with Alligator Shooting for Variety." *Field and Stream*. March 1904. Vol. 8, no. 11.

111. Kimball, Art and Scott. *Early Fishing Plugs of the U.S.A.* Boulder Junction, WI: Aardvark Publications, 1989. ISBN 0-9604906-8-X.

112. Heddon, James. "Black Bass in Florida." *Magazine Angling Stories*. Prior to 1915, when recorded in the Harvard Library as a gift of Daniel B. Fearing, class of 1882. Compilation of early nineteenth-century angling stories from popular periodicals.

113. McClane, A. J. "Performing Arts." *Field & Stream*. October 1971.

114. Lucas, Jason. "A Weedless Lure That Isn't Fishless." *Sports Afield*. March 1968.

115. Brasher, Keith (owner and operator of War Eagle Custom Lures, Rogers, Arkansas). Interview with Emmett Babler. April 6, 2016.

116. Harold E. Smith, M.D. *Collector's Encyclopedia of Creek Chub*. 2nd ed. Paducah, KY: Collector Books, 2002.

117. Ohio History Connection. "Rubber Industry." *Ohio History Central* [online]. [Accessed April 8, 2016.] http://www.ohiohistorycentral.org/w/Rubber_Industry?rec=1533.

118. C. L. Dowell. *Bulletin 6408—Dams and Reservoirs in Texas: Historical and Descriptive Information*. Texas Water Development Board. Austin: Texas Water Commission, 1964, pp. 253–267.

119. Rapala VMC Corporation. "Our History" [online]. [Accessed April 10, 2016.] http://www.rapala.com/content/rapala-general-information/our-history.html.

120. "Rapala History." *Rapala World News* [online]. April 2011. [Accessed April 10, 2016.] http://rapalaworld.blogspot.com/2011/04/lauri-rapala.html. Unofficial Rapala website created and supported by Rapala fans.

121. Rapala VMC Corporation. "Decisions of Rapala VMC Corporation's Annual General Meeting on April 1, 2016." Available at http://www.rapalavmc.com/investors/annual-general-meeting-2016.

122. Gayle Reels, Ltd. *The Gayle Reels of Kentucky.* Circa 2004. A spiral-bound booklet that appears to have been written by the Gayle family or persons closely associated with the family. Three testimonials on the last page are all dated 2004.

123. Gayle, Currey. Interviews with Emmett Babler. December 2016. Currey Gayle, the great-grandson of Clarence Gayle, is the family historian and tackle collector.

124. "Gayle Reel History." *Gayle Reels* [online]. [Accessed March 8, 2016.] http://www.gaylereels.com/history.htm.

125. "Clarence Gayle Awarded Contract by Government." *The State Journal* (Frankfort, KY). November 11, 1918.

126. Fuss, John C. "Industrial Frankfort, and Entertainment." *The State Journal* (Frankfort, KY). October 10, 1976, p. 22.

127. Niles, Rena. "Fishing Reels to Atom Bombs." *The Courier-Journal Roto-Magazine* (Louisville, KY). September 16, 1945, p. 13.

128. Caywood, D. T. "Behind the Scenes with Kentucky Sportsmen, No. 1 in a Series of Personality Sketches on Sportsmen Worth Knowing—Clarence W. Gayle, Maker of Fine Fishing Reels." *The Kentucky Sportsman.* April 1946.

129. Hawes, Harry B. *My Friend the Black Bass.* New York: Frederick A. Stokes Company, 1930.

130. Bergman, Ray. *With Fly, Plug, and Bait.* New York: William Morrow & Company, 1947.

131. Owens Corning Corporation. "Key Historical Milestones" [online]. [Accessed March 23, 2016.] http://media.owenscorning.com/history.

132. Shedd, Dennis, District Court Judge. *Shakespeare Co. v. Silstar Corp.* Civ. A. No. 3:90-1695-19, September 24, 1992: US District Court, District of South Carolina, 1992.

133. "Shakespeare's History." *America Goes Fishing with Shakespeare* [online]. 2013. [Accessed March 21, 2016.] https://mpf.shakespeare-fishing.com/history/index.shtml.

134. US General Services Administration. "Nickel Silver: Characteristics, Uses and Problems" [online]. [Accessed March 25, 2016.] http://www.gsa.gov/portal/content/113754.

135. "The Discovery of Stainless Steel." *British Stainless Steel Association* [online]. [Accessed March 25, 2016.] http://www.bssa.org.uk/about_stainless_steel.php?id=31.

136. "Aluminium History." *All About Aluminium* [online]. [Accessed March 25, 2016.] http://www.aluminiumleader.com/history/industry_history.

137. "Monofilament Fishing Lines." *Sufix* [online]. [Accessed March 21, 2016.] http://sufix.fishing/monofilament-fishing-lines.

138. DuPont Corporation. "DuPont Heritage Timeline" [online]. [Accessed March 23, 2016.] http://www.dupont.com/corporate-functions/our-company/dupont-history.html.

139. ———. "DuPont Heritage Timeline" [online]. [Accessed March 23, 2016.] http://www2.dupont.com/Phoenix_Heritage/en_US/1929_a_detail.html.

140. Stren Fishing Lines. "About Stren" [online]. [Accessed March 23, 2016.] http://www.stren.com/Stren-about-stren.html.

141. Vernon, Steven K. *Antique Fishing Reels.* Harrisburg: Stackpole Books, 1985, pp. 10, 14. ISBN 0-8117-0108-5.

142. Hutton, Thomas Hubert, and Blake, Stanley. *The Complete Angler and Huntsman.* Berry, KY: n.p., 1919, p. 265.

143. Creel, Mike. "Watchmaker's Reel." *Kentucky Happy Hunting Ground.* March-April 1980.

144. Wattenberg, Ben J., and the US Bureau of the Census. *The Statistical History of the United States, From Colonial Times to 1970*. New York: Basic Books, 1976. Introduction and user's guide by Wattenberg. ISBN 0-465-08203-3.

145. Doggett, Joe. "The Red Reel." *Field and Stream*. June 25, 2002.

146. Sills, Joe. "A Reel That's Nearly Impossible to Backlash Leads Diawa's New Bass Pack." *Fishing Tackle Retailer*. March 30, 2016.

147. Masters, A. William. "Outing with a Portable Equipment." *American Homes and Gardens*. July 1911.

148. Acme Folding Boat Co. "Klondike Special" (advertisement). *Harpers New Monthly Magazine*. New York, London: Harper & Brothers, May 1900.

149. Blodgett, Thos. H. "The Motor Boat In Sport." *Field and Stream*. 1904.

150. Schnurmacher, E. C. (Doc). *Practical Outboard Motorboat Building and Operation*. New York: Outboard Motorboat, 1930.

151. "The Ford of Water Sports." *Outing*. April 1919, pp. 50–53.

152. Carroll, Dixie. *Fishing, Tackle and Kits*. Cincinnati: Stewart & Kidd, 1919, pp. 289–290.

153. "Johnson Outboards 1922—The Beginning Years." *Yankee Chapter, Antique Outboard Motor Club* [online]. [Accessed April 13, 2016.] http://www.yankeeaomci.org/johnsonat85.htm.

154. "The 1909 Johnson Monoplane—Years Ahead of Its Time." *Contact*. Issue 9, pp. 9–12. *The Australian Vintage Aviation Society (TAVAS)* [online]. [Accessed April 14, 2016.] http://www.eaa83.org/hd/The_Johnson_Monoplane.pdf.

155. Boyt, Lee. "The History of Bass Boats, Bass and Walleye Boats." *USA Outdoors* [online]. 2006. [Accessed April 17, 2016.] http://www.usaoutdoors.org/f228/little-bass-boat-history-1153.html.

156. "Men Who Changed the Way We Fish." *Game & Fish* [online]. September 24, 2010. [Accessed April 17, 2016.] http://www.gameandfishmag.com/fishing/fishing_ra_changefish_0210.

157. *Skeeter: Action-Packed Fiberglass Boats for Every Sportsman.* Longview, TX: Stemco Manufacturing Company, 1962. Product catalog.

158. Rhude, Andreas Jordahl. "Larson Boats: A Minnesota Institution." *The Antique and Classic Boat Society, Bob Speltz Land-O-Lakes Chapter* [online]. [Accessed April 17, 2016.] http://acbs-bslol.com/boating-history/boatbuilders/larsonbwpt2.

159. "Lund Boat Company Founder Dies at 91." *In Depth Outdoors* [online]. October 24, 2003. [Accessed April 17, 2016.] https://www.in-depthoutdoors.com/community/forums/topic/ftlgeneral_69525.

160. Monsour, Theresa. "Howard Lund Dies." *St. Paul Pioneer Press.* 2003.

161. "Father of Hobie Mirage Drive Greg Ketterman." *Kayak Angler* blog. August 1, 2013. [Accessed April 17, 2016.] http://journalsblog.com/kayak-angler/kayak-angler-august-1-2013/2736-father-of-hobie-mirage-drive-greg-ketterman.html.

162. Thomson, Elizabeth A. "'Penguin Boat' Plies the Charles." *MIT News* [online]. April 3, 1997. [Accessed April 18, 2016.] http://news.mit.edu/1997/penguin-0403.

163. Baits, Joseph D., Jr. *Spinning for American Game Fish.* Boston: Little, Brown and Company, 1947.

164. Ovington, Raymond W., Jr. *Spinning in America.* Harrisburg, PA: Stackpole, 1954. Library of Congress no. 54-8684.

165. Fox, Charles K. *Advanced Baitcasting.* New York: G. P. Putnam's Sons, 1950.

165. Koller, Larry. *The Complete Book of Fishing Tackle.* Indianapolis and New York: Bobbs-Merrill, 1955.

167. Liotta, Ernest Jr. *The Technique of Bait Casting.* (Little Sports Library.) Chicago, New York, Los Angeles: Ziff Davis, 1949.

# A TRIBUTE TO STANLEY FAGERSTROM

Stan, a decorated combat veteran of World War II, helped launch modern bass fishing in America's western states as both an angler and writer following the war. No one has written more about western bass fishing than Stan.

A lifelong angler, Stan began his writing career upon his return from the war's South Pacific theater, where, as an Army sergeant in Company G, 167th Infantry, 31st Infantry Division, he served through almost two years of fierce jungle fighting. Tom Hanks and Gary Sinise, stars of the movie Forrest Gump and advocates for recognition of vets, have personally honored Stan for his service in the campaign for Mindanao in the Philippine Islands, so profoundly expressed in Stan's poem "No Second Chance."

Stan is also a star of instructional casting videos. He has earned his nickname "The Master Caster" by performing casting demonstrations internationally since 1952.

In 1971 Stan was the only writer from the Pacific Northwest invited to Lake Mead to participate as an observer in the very first Bassmasters Classic, an annual tournament whose winner is widely considered the world champion of bass fishing. Stan attended all but two of the first thirty Classics. For several years, he also demonstrated his casting prowess at the Classic Outdoor Show. He was named a lifetime honorary member of the Oregon Bass & Panfish Club, a respected organization headquartered in Portland. Stan was the winner for all five years in which he participated in the club's annual contest for catching the year's largest bass.

In 2000 Stan was inducted as a member of the National Freshwater Fishing Hall of Fame, and in 2001 the National Professional Anglers Association presented him with an honorary lifetime membership award. In 2007 the Bass Fishing Hall of Fame inducted Stan into its esteemed ranks. To understand what an honor that is, it is helpful to know that a man Stan considers one of the fathers of bass fishing—his old friend and former angling editor of Sports Afield magazine, Jason Lucas—has yet to receive an induction.

Stan maintains that Homer Circle, another great writer and angler who gave special meaning to the term "friend," had much to do with his invitation to the first Bassmasters Classic. Circle, angling editor of Sports Afield magazine for thirty-five years and prominent television host of numerous fishing shows, inspired Stan by providing him with more opportunities to write. Because of Circle's influence, Stan was appointed to the Braniff Outdoor Council. Homer and Stan, while traveling together for the Outdoor Council, eventually shared a boat together in many places around the globe, including Stan's home lake in Washington State; Circle's home lake in Ocala, Florida; Alaska; the Amazon; and Colombia, South America, where they fished for baby tarpon. Stan, always one to recognize life's possibilities, made the most of them. At this writing, angling is a better sport because of Stan and Homer's friendship.

A poet, award-winning outdoor writer, and author of four books, Stan has penned thousands of articles for many of America's premier sporting publications, newspaper columns, and Internet sites. They stand as an inheritance for American anglers who choose to improve their sport and themselves.

Stan always answers the call, whether in service to his country or to individual souls that his life path crosses. Stan is a man of love who accepts responsibility for doing what needs to be done to make things in this world better and more reflective of the full glory of its origin. He lives and shares his life that way—in communion with God and his neighbor.

# Index

**Note:** Page numbers in italics denote references to photographs.

ABU Corporation, 136
Acme Folding Boat Company, 142
Agnel, H. R., 38–39
Alumacraft Boat Company, 150
aluminum, 123
aluminum boats, 149–150, 153
Ambassadeur 2000 reel, 136–37
*The American Angler's Guide*
(Brown), 45–48
*American Fishing Books* (Wetzel), 53
American Fork and Hoe Company, 119
angler's character vs. fish's attributes,
72–73
*Angling in America* (Goodspeed), 7,
53, 77
angling kayaks, 151–52
angling methods. *See* baitcasting;
spincasting; spinning method;
still-fishing
angling spoons, 48, 49, 50, 51, 90
anti-backlash device, 129–131
*Antique Fishing Reels* (Vernon), 129
Arbogast, Fred, 86, 119
arc-bottom hull, 147–48
Arnold, Henry H. "Hap," 113
artificial lures. *See* lures
artificial worm, 100–102
Artistic Minnow, 88, 88
*The Art of Angling* (Holberton), 60
"The Art of Bait Casting" (article), 87
The Art of Bait-Casting (pamphlet), 85
Ayers, Samuel, 22
Ayres, Thomas Robinson Jameson, 22

backlash, 127, 129, 137
backlash-free reel, 139
baitcasters, influential, 60–66
baitcast finesse system, 158
baitcasting. *See also* baitcasting
system

adaptability of, 77
artificial lures (*See* lures)
backlash and, 127
fly-fishing vs., 77
with live bait, 57–60
as a national sport, 60, 66, 89
reels for (*See* casting reels)
rods for (*See* rods, fishing)
spincasting reels, 136–37
spinning method, 134–35
standard equipment for, 79
still-fishing and, 19
Van Buren's tackle, 64, 65
baitcasting method, 59–60, 127–29
baitcasting system
balanced, 85–86
definition of, 79
detachable rod handle, 119–120
fiberglass and, 121–22
fishing line, 124–25
hollow-steel rods, 120
lures, 94, 100, 157–58
new metals and alloys changing,
123–24
rod as foundation for, 83–84
steel rods, 117–19
bamboo rods, 53, 117
bass. *See also* bass fishing
abundance in Kentucky, 14
adaptability of, 37
diet for, 15
eating habits of, 15
principal food for, 50
redistribution of, 37
still-fishing to catch, 15
transplanting, 37–39
at Woods Lake, 38–39
Bass Anglers Sportsman's Society
(BASS), 137
bass boats, 148–49
bass fishing
as an art, 14
earliest record of, 9–10

early defense of, 7
game worthiness of fish species, 69
gigging, 75
at Lake Gogebic Michigan, vi
morality of, 7
net fishing, 74–75
recreational, 4–6, 11
states regulating, 71–73, 76
Bass Fishing Hall of Fame, 175
Bassmasters Classic, 175
bass rods, 53
bass tournaments, 95–96, 159
Battle of Buena Vista, 35–36
B.C. Milam, Frankfort, KY (trade name), 28
B.C. Milam & Son reels, 28, 32
Bergman, Ray, 120
Bethabara wood baitcasting rod, 82
B.F. Meek, Louisville, KY (trade name), 29
B.F. Meek & Sons, 29
B.F. Meek No. 3 reel, 30
black bass. *See* bass
*Black Bass Fishing: Theory and Practice* (Lincoln), 84
Blackstone River, 33–34
Blair, Francis Preston, Sr., 62, 62, 65
boats. *See* watercraft
*Book of Sports*, 1–2
*Book of the Black Bass* (Henshall), 14, 25–26, 57–58, 66, 81
Boone, Daniel, 13
braided fishing line, 124
braided raw silk fishing line, 125
Braniff Outdoor Council, 175
Brashers, Keith, 98
Brearley, Harry, 123
Brown, Bache Hamilton, 155
Brown, John, 22
Brown, John J., 45
Brown, Mason, 22, 23, 62, 62, 68
Brown, Orlando, Jr., 68
Brunswick, 149
Buel, Julio Thompson, 48, 49
Buel spoons, 48, 49, 50, 51

Calcutta bamboo fishing rods, 41
cane rods, 15–16
Carnegie, Andrew, 40
Carothers, Wallace Hume, 125
Carroll, Dixie, 145, 150, 154
Carter, Arlan, 49
Carver Snyder reel, 18–19, 18
Cary, Bess, 144
casting. *See* baitcasting; casting reels; fly-casting; minnow casting
casting lures. *See* lures
casting reels. *See also* Kentucky reel
  with anti-backlash device, 129–131
  anti-backlash device, 129
  centrifugal brakes for, 138
  with combination brakes, 139
  description of, 127–29
  Frankfort Kentucky Reel, 28–31, 43, 60
  Gayle reels, 106–9, 107, 111
  handmade, 18–19, 42
  Kentucky multiplying, 54, 58
  with level-winding mechanisms, 132
  machine-made, 42–43
  magnetic brakes for, 138–39
  multiplying, 16
  New York reel, 64
  No. 3 General Utility model, 32
  No. 3 reel, B.F. Meek, 30
  No. 4 reel, B.C. Milam, 55
  parts of, 128
  producing, 16–17
  Redifor Self-Thumbing, 130, 130
  reel brakes, 130–31, 138–39
  reel spool weight, 86–87
  Rustic, 32
  Shakespeare Marhoff model, 123–24
  single-action, 16
  Snyder reel, 18–19, 18, 157
  South Bend 1131-A, 130, 130
  value-priced line of, 133–34
casting technique
  overhead cast, 84
  side-arm casting, 84, 88–89
  underhand, 81
casting tournaments, 85–86

Castle (Fishing Company's clubhouse), 5, 5
centrifugal brakes, 138
Charles I, King of England, 1–2, 155
Cherokee Nation, 13
Chicago bass angling, 80–81
Chicago Fly Casting Club, 83, 107
Chubb, Thomas H., 39–41
Chubb's Black Bass Reel, 41, 43
Circle, Homer, 175
Clarke, J. M., 82, 91
Clay, Henry, 63, 63, 64
Cleveland, Grover, 44
Clinton Engineer Works, 112
Coaxer, 94, 94, 96
Coaxer lure, 94–95, 94
Columbian Exposition, World's Fair, 43
"The Coming Black Bass Rod" (Henshall), 80
commercial fish harvesting activities, 74
*The Compleat Angler* (Walton), 2–3
*The Complete Angler and Huntsman* (Hutton), 131
Comstock, Harry, 91
Connecticut, first English settlement in, 3
Connecticut River, 3–4
Cook, Rose, 140, 150
Cooney, John, 64
Corinthian Capital Group LLC, 150
Creek Chub Bait Company (CCBC), 98, 99
Creme, Nick and Cosma, 94, 100–102
Crestliner Boats, 149
Czarnowski, James, 151

Dacron fishing line, 125
Dame, Stoddard & Kendall, 53
Dardevle spoon, 49
Darling, Lou S., 86
Decker, Anson B. "Anse," 95–96
Decker Surface Water Casting Bass Bait, 96
de Lafayette, Marquis, 4
Denison, Warren, 136

Denison Johnson Model 20 Sidewinder, 136
Dills, Henry, 99
Divine, Fred D., 82
diving lip, 99–100
Dowagiac Expert Perfect Surface Casting Bait lure, 92–93
Dowagiac Minnow No. 20, 88
Dowagiac No. 2, 92
Dowagiac Underwater, 92
downstream vertical integration, 41
DuPont, 101, 125

E. I. du Pont de Nemours and Company, 125
Elto, 146
English reel, 16
Eppinger Manufacturing Company, 49
Evinrude, Ole, 144–46
Evinrude Light Twin Outboard, 146
Evinrude outboard motor, 144–46

Fagerstrom, Stanley, 174–75
fairy wand, 83, 84
F. H. Lawson Company, 112
fiberglass, 121–22
fiberglass boats, 148
*Field & Stream* magazine, 95–96
finesse fishing, 158
fin-powered prototype boat, 151–52
*Fish and Fishing* (Herbert), 70
Fisheries Pavilion at Chicago World's Fair, 43
*Fishing in American Waters* (Scott), 52
fishing line, 124–25
fishing line dryers, 125
*Fishing Reel Makers of Kentucky* (Vernon and Stewart), 18, 28
fishing reels. See reels, fishing
fishing tackle. See tackle
fish's attributes vs. anglers character, 72–73
flat-bottom hulls, 147
floating/diving lure, 98–100
Florida, purchase of, 35
fly-casting, 69, 70

fly-fishing, bait angling vs., 77
Flying Hellgrammite, 91
folding boat, 142–43
Forester, Frank (pen name), 70
Fort Johnson, 8
Fox, Charlie, 157
Foxcroft, Thomas, 3
Frankfort Kentucky Reel, 28–31, 43, 60. *See also* Kentucky reel
freshwater fishing boats, 141–43
Fresh Water Pond (New York City), 6
friction-free line guide, 139
Frog-Casting rod, 81
F. W. Woolworth Company, 109

Game and Fish Commission of Minnesota, 71, 73
game fish, 69–70
*Game Fish of Northern States* (Roosevelt), 50
game worthiness of fish species, 69
Garber, Paul, 146
Gayle, Clarence. *See also* Gayle reels
  birth of, 105
  Buick Motors and, 108
  building Sea Sled-type watercraft, 113–14
  death of, 115
  F.W. Woolworth Company and, 109
  government subcontract work for, 111–13
  on handmade vs. machine-made reels, 42–43
  as Harley Davidson machinist, 108
  photograph of, 106, 115
  producing artificial lures, 109–10
  resuming production, 111
  use of aluminum, 123
Gayle, Coburn, 112
Gayle, Currey, 110
Gayle, Emma (Kavanaugh), 109, 114
Gayle, George William, 105
Gayle, Joe A. "Shorty," 109, 113
Gayle, Sadie, 106
Gayle Aluminum Trout Reel, 111

Gayle reels
  first, 106
  Intrinsic model, 107, 107, 108
  Simplicity line, 108–9
  V. L. & A. pattern, 108
George William Gayle & Son Company, 105
Geo. W. Gayle & Son, 111
German silver, 123
Gibbs, Oliver, 71
gigging, 75
Golden Age of tackle manufacturing, 41, 89
Goodspeed, Charles Eliot, 7, 53, 77
Great Britain, 1
great leap westward, 34–35
Grissom, Herbert, 81, 83–84
gunsmiths, 17
gutta-percha plastic, 51

Hackle, Sparse Grey, 39, 66
handmade reels, 18–19, 42, 107, 115
Hanks, Tom, 175
Hardman, Jacob Wolf, 25–27
Hardman reels, 25–26, 26
Harley, James, 92
Harris, Charlie, 92
Harris frog lure, 92
Haskell, Riley, 52
Haskell minnow, 52, 91
Hawes, Harry B., 119
Heddon, James, 92, 95
Heddon, John, 87
Heddon, William, 92
Heinzerling, Carl, 99
Henderson, Richard, 13
Henshall, James Alexander
  announcing new type of fishing rod, 80
  background of, 14–15
  on bait fishermen, 17
  distributing Book of the Black Bass, 66
  minnow casting, 57–58
  photograph of, 67
  on short rods, 81
  still-fishing technique of, 79

Henshall Rod, 80–84
Henshall Van Antwerp black bass reel, 41
Herbert, Henry William, 70
Hickman, William Albert, 113
Hobie Cat Company, 152
Hobie Mirage Drive, 152, 153
Holmes, William, 3
homemade reels, 16
Horton, Everett, 117
Horton Manufacturing Company, 117
Hough, Emerson, 80–81, 82
Howald, Arthur, 121
*How to Catch Game Fish* (Lamb), 89
Hull, Jasper R. Dell, 136
hull design, 147–48
Hunter, Robert, Jr., 10
Hutton, Thomas Hubert, 131

imitation fish, 51–52
industrialization, 33–34
Industrial Revolution
    effects on fish, 34
    railroads, 36
    textile mills, 33–34
    vertical integration and, 40–41
    western expansion in, 36
Inland Marine Corporation, 149–150

J. A. Coxe 25-3 reel, 128
James Heddon & Son, 87, 92–93, 120
James I, King of England, 1
Jamison, William, 85–86, 95
J.F. Meek & Co., 28
John J. Brown & Co.'s Angler's Dept and General Emporium, 45
Johnson, Harry, 146–47
Johnson, John, 7, 9–10, 10
Johnson, Julius, 146–47
Johnson, Karl E., 2
Johnson, Lloyd, 136
Johnson, Lou, 146–47
Johnson, William, 7–9, 8
Johnson Century 100 reel, 136
Johnson Hall, 9, 9
Johnson Town, 9

Kavanaugh, Emma. *See* Gayle, Emma (Kavanaugh)
kayaks, 151–52
Kentucky
    anglers from, 14–16
    Mexican-American war heroes of, 35–36
    population of, 13
    purchase of, 13
    water transportation corridors, 14
Kentucky reel. *See also* Frankfort
Kentucky Reel
    for bait casting, 58
    demand for, 18
    Gayle producing, 107
    improvements to, 25–26
    for long casting, 80–81
    materials used for, 123
    metals and alloys used, 123
    Sage on, 32
Ketterman, Dan, 151
Ketterman, Greg, 151, 152
Knox, John, 3

laid fishing line, 124
Lamb, Jack, 89
large-lure systems, 157
Larson, Paul, 149
Larson Boat Works, 149
Larson Watercraft, 149
lay-out line, 5
leisure activities, restrictions on, 2
level-winding mechanism, 129, 132
light-line fishing, 158
light-lure casting system, 158
Lincoln, Robert Page, 84, 96, 110–11, 119–120, 156
Lindenwald, 64
line, fishing, 124–25
Liotta, Ernest, Jr., 158
Louisiana Purchase, 34
Loyalist anglers, 7–10
Lucas, Jason, 98
Lund, G. Howard, 149–150
Lund Metal Craft, 150

lures
Artistic Minnow, 88
Coaxer, 94, 94
Decker Surface Water Casting
Bass Bait, 96
development and innovation, 94–95
with diving lip, 99–100
Dowagiac Minnow No. 20, 88
Draw 'Em All lure, 110
floating/diving, 98–100
Flying Hellgrammite, 91
Gayle lures, 109–10, 110
Harris frog lure, 92
Haskell Minnow, 52
hook-laden, heavy, 87–88
natural baits, 95
No. 100 Wiggler, 94, 98–100,
99, 100
Original Floating Wobbler, 94,
102–3, 102
Phantom Minnow, 51–52, 52
plug, 91
pork, 95
revolving-head surface, 96
Roosevelt on, 51
Shorty lure, 109
spinning-type, 90
spoon-type, 90
surface, 92–93
surface/diving types, 109
Texas Rigged Worm, 101
Trout Bait No. 83, 51–52
Twin Spinner, 94, 97
underwater, 92
weight-buoy, 88
Wiggle Worm, 94, 100–102
wooden, 91, 92
wooden frog, 92
Woods Expert Minnow, 91
lure weights, 85–88, 95, 158

Macy, Bill, 96
magnetic brakes, 138–39
Marhoff reels, 123–24
marine propulsion systems, 151–52
Marshall, Humphrey, 35

Martin Van Buren National Historical
Site, 64
Mary I, Queen of England, 3
mass production, 39, 41, 42
Mayflower voyage, 2
McCarthy, Ms. J.G., 56
McClaine, A. J., 96
Meek, Benjamin Franklin, 22–23,
28–30, 29, 42, 106
Meek, Jonathan Fleming, 22–24, 27
Meek, Pitman, 29
Meek, Sylvanus, 29
Meek & Milam (trade name), 28
Meek Brothers, 22–24
Meyer, Chris, 145
midget plugging, 157. See also
plugging
Milam, Benjamin Cave
as apprentice to Beverly Noel, 23
as apprentice to J.F. Meek, 23–24
death of, 31
false advertising lawsuit, 30
handmade reels and, 42
in Mexican-American war, 35
photograph of, 29, 35
use of treadle, 42
as watchmaker, 28
Milam, John W., 28, 30, 31, 32
Miller, Alfred W., 39, 157
Miller, Shackelford, 30–31
Minnesota, 71, 72
minnow casting, 57–60
Mirage Drive, 152, 153
Model B reel, 132, 133
Mohawk nation, 8
Mohawk River, 8–9
monofilament fishing line, 125
monoplanes, 146
multiplying reels. See casting reels;
Kentucky reel
My Friend the Black Bass
(Hawes), 119

National Association of Scientific
Angling Clubs (NASAC), 85–86
National Professional Anglers

Association, 175
natural baits, 95
net fishing, 74–75
New York City, angling laws in, 6–7
New York City Common Council, 6–7
New York reel, 64
New York State Fishery
Commission, 75
nickel silver, 123
*19th Century Fishing Lures*
(Carter), 49
No. 3 General Utility model reel, 32
No. 3 reel, B.F. Meek, 30
No. 4 reel, B.C. Milam, 55
No. 100 Wiggler, 94, 98–100, 99, 100
No. 100 Worm lure, 94
Noel, Beverly, 23
Noel, Theodore, 19, 23
Norris, Thaddeus, 50, 53–54, 70, 77
novice anglers, 77, 88–89, 136
Nowell, Alexander, 2–3
nylon fishing line, 125
*Ocean* (steamboat), 24
Oregon Territory, 35
Original Floating Wobbler, 94,
102–3, 102
O. Ustonson, Maker to His Majesty
Temple Bar London reel, 16
outboard motors, 50, 144–48
overhead cast, 82, 84
Ovington, Ray, 156
Owens-Corning Fiberglas Corp, 121

Palmer, Mark S., 132
Patrick, Ebenezer, 27
Peak, Frank, 92
Penn, William, 4
Pflueger Supreme reel, 133, 134
Phantom Minnow, 51–52, 52, 91
Philippe, Samuel, 53
plugging, 157
plug lures, 91–93
plumb line, 5–6
Plymouth Colony, 2, 3
polyester fishing line, 125
population growth in United States,
33–34

pork lures, 95
*Problematizing Puritan Play* study, 2
Proteus, 151–52
Puritan anglers, 2–3
Puritanism, 2–3

quadruple multiplier, 129

railways
   angling interest and, 36–37
   bass redistribution project, 37
   facilitating western expansion, 36
   onboard water supply, 37
Rapala, Lauri, 102–3
Rapala VMC Corporation, 103
rapier steel rods, 118, 118
recreation, Puritan definition of, 2–3
recreational fishing, 4–6, 11
Redifor Beetzsel reel, 133, 134
Redifor Self-Thumbing reel, 130, 130
reel brakes, 130–31, 137–39
reels, fishing. *See* casting reels

reel spool weight, effect of, 86–87
Reeves Marine, 148
regulations over fishing activities, 71
Revolutionary War, angling after, 11
revolving-head surface lures, 96
Rhead, Louis
   illustration, 145, 153, 159
   woodcut, 126
Ripley, Ozark, 87, 117
Rodman, Edmund, 112
Rodman, Moraih, 27
rods, fishing
   balance handle, 54
   bamboo, 53, 117
   bass, 53
   Bethabara wood baitcasting, 82
   cane, 15–16
   detachable rod handle, 119–120
   fiberglass, 121–22
   Frog-Casting, 81
   graphite, 122
   hollow, 121
   rapier steel, 118, 118
   seamless tubular steel, 120

short, 81–84, 84
Short Bait Casting, 82
solid, 121
solid steel baitcasting, 119
split bamboo, 53
steel baitcasting, 117–18, 120
Wonder Rod, 122

Roosevelt, Robert Barnwell, 50, 51,
74–76, 77, 78
Roosevelt, Theodore, 34, 74, 76
round-bottom hulls, 147
Rustic reel, 32

Sage, James L., 21–25, 27, 32
Schulthess, George, 99
The Schuylkill Fishing Company of the
Colony in Schuylkill fishing club, 4
Scientific Angling Tournament, 95,
107, 108
Scull, Benjamin, 5
Sea Sled, 113
Sea Sled Emma K 4, 113
Seccombe, Joseph, 7

*A Serious Address to Those Who
Unnecessarily Frequent the Tavern*
(homily), 3
Shakespeare, William, Jr., 85
Shakespeare Company
   date codes, 124, 124
   fiberglass rods, 121
   Marhoff reel, 123–24
   Model B reel, 132, 133
   one-piece handle, 120
   Rustic reel, 32
   Ugly Stik, 122
Shannon, Jesse P., 98
Shannon Tackle Corporation, 98
Shannon Twin Spinner. *See* Twin
Spinner
Shell Lake Boat Company, 150
Short Bait Casting rod, 82
short rod, 80–84, 84
Shorty lure, 109

Shriver, W. W., 37
side-arm casting, 84, 88–89
silk fishing line, 125
single-action click reel, 59–60
Siniese, Gary, 175
slack-water navigation, 24
Slater textile mill, 33, 33
smallmouth bass. *See* bass
Smith, O. W., 133
Smith Age of tackle manufacturing,
41, 89
Snyder, Charles, 18
Snyder, David M., 57
Snyder, George, 17–19
Snyder, John, 18
Snyder, R. J., 19
Snyder reel, 18–19, 18, 157
social class, transcending, 1
solid steel baitcasting rods, 119
South Bend 1131-A reel, 130, 130, 131
spearing, 75
spincasting, 1, 155–56
spincasting reels, 77, 136–37, 157
spinner baits, 98
*Spinning in America* (Ovington), 156
spinning method, 134–35, 155–56
split bamboo rod, 53

spoons, angling, 48, 49, 50, 51, 90
sport angler, 77
sport fishing method. *See* baitcasting;
spincasting; spinning method
stainless steel, 123
steamboats, 24–25
steam-powered paddle craft, 143
Steelback lures, 110
steel baitcasting rods, 117–19, 120
steel production, 40
Stemco, 148
stern-mounted gas engines, 144
Stewart, Frank M., III, 16, 18, 28
still-fishing
   baitcasting and, 19
   fishing line for, 124
   with Kentucky reel, 58

with minnows, 58
  Silverside's method, 58–59
  Snyder's reel and, 58
  technique of, 15–16
Stren monofilament fishing line, 125
*Superior Fishing* (Roosevelt), 48, 51
Super Skeeter, 148
surface lures, 92–93

tackle. *See also* lures; reels, fishing;
  rods, fishing
  for bait casting, 85
  Brown's recommended, 46–47
  Buel spoons, 48, 49, 50, 51
  Dardevle spoon, 49
  of Martin Van Buren, 64, 65
  mass-producing, 39
  trolling-spoon lures, 48
  weedless hook, 49
tackle manufacturing, 39–41
Tanner, Lent, 106
telescoping rods, 117
Texas Rigged Worm, 101
Texas Water Commission, 101
textile mills, 33–34
T. H. Chubb Rod Co., 40
Thommen Record spinning reel, 135
Thompson, John B., 87
Thurman, Holmes, 148
Toledo Bend Dam and Reservoir, 101
Tooley, Lloyd J., 85
Tooley Tackle Company, 85
Top Hat raised gearbox reel, 107, 111
*Tournament Casting and the Proper
Equipment* (Darling), 86
tournament competition events,
85–86, 159
trailer boats, 149–150
treadle, 42
Treaty of Sycamore Shoals, 13
TriFoiler sailboat, 151
trolling, 46, 50, 53, 70, 143, 153
trolling minnows, 91
trolling-spoon lures, 48, 49
Trout Bait No. 83, 51–52
true angler, qualities of, 70
True Temper, 119, 120
twin-cylinder engine, 145–46

Twin Spinner, 94, 97, 98
Twin Spinner lure, 94
twisted fishing line, 124

underwater lures, 92
upstream vertical integration, 40
US Fish and Wildlife Service, 75–76
US Fish Commission, 75

Van Buren, Martin, 63, 63, 64, 65
V-bottom hulls, 147
Vernon, Steven K., 18, 129
vertical integration, 40–41
Von Lengerke & Antoine, 108

Walton, Izaak, 2–3
War Eagle spinner bait, 98
Washington, George, 4, 11, 116
watercraft
  aluminum, 149–150, 153
  bass fishing, 148–49
  fiberglass, 148
  fin-powered, 151–52
  kayaks, 151–52
  trailer, 149–150
  TriFoiler sailboat, 151
weedless hook, 49
Wetzel, Charles M., 53
Wiggle Worm, 94, 100–102
William Mills & Son, 108
*With Fly, Plug, and Bait*
(Bergman), 120
W. J. Jamison Company, 98
Wold, Robert H., 149
Wonder Rod, 122
wooden frog lure, 92
wooden plug lure, 92
Woods Expert Minnow, 91
Woods Lake, 38–39
World War II, 112

Zass, W. B., 119
Zebco 33 reel, 136
Zebco Standard reel, 136
Zero Hour Bomb Company (Zebco)
standard reel, 136

# ABOUT THE AUTHOR

Emmett Babler is a lifelong angler and fishing tackle historian.
A US Navy veteran, he holds two undergraduate degrees and a master
of arts in human relations and organizational behavior. He is a retired
Honeywell Aerospace director, a retired clergy member of the Episcopal
Church, a multimedia artisan, writer and an aspiring swing dancer.
Emmett and his wife, Carmela live in Arizona and have six
grandchildren.

Made in the USA
Columbia, SC
25 October 2020